D1109122

T2-BVE-307

2/00 20/00 (11/98)
7/96-17-11/95
5/94-13 (4-94)

DOWNTOWN BRANCH
Palo Alto City Library

The individual borrower is responsible for all library material borrowed on his card.

Charges as determined by the CITY OF PALO ALTO will be assessed for each overdue item.

Damaged or non-returned property will be billed to the individual borrower by the CITY OF PALO ALTO.

20M 11/78

Stamp Collecting

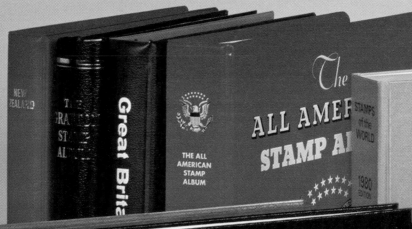

NEW ZEALAND

THE GRAFTON STAMP ALBUM

Great Britain

THE ALL AMERICAN STAMP ALBUM

The ALL AMERICAN STAMP ALBUM
1980 EDITION

STAMPS of the WORLD

STAMPS of the WORLD 1980

A Stanley Gibbons

Der farbige Taschenkatalog

MICH
JUNIOR-KATALOG MIT SAARLAND

Australi

RAPKINS

Sta

LEY GIBBONS
P CATALOGUE

Part 1
British Commonwea

FAC
SPECIALKATAL

ÍSLAND
NORGE
DANMARK

FRIMÄRKSHUSE

CATALOGUE
YVERT ET

1980 TOME
TIMBRE
Europa
Pays d'express
Andorre
Afrique du Nor
Monaco
Sarre

VOL. 3

SCOTT
1980 standard postage stamp catalogue
Countries of the World
G-O

STA
STANLEY
STAMP C
Part 7

STANLEY GIBBONS STAMP COLOUR KEY

Philatector

Stamp Collecting

James Mackay

VNR VAN NOSTRAND REINHOLD COMPANY
NEW YORK CINCINNATI TORONTO LONDON MELBOURNE

Text Copyright © 1980 by James Mackay
Library of Congress Catalog Card Number 82-50854
ISBN 0-442-26315-5

All rights reserved. No part of this work covered by the copyright hereon
may be reproduced or used in any form or by any means – graphic, electronic,
or mechanical, including photocopying, recording, taping, or information storage
and retrieval systems – without written permission of the publisher.

Printed in Hong Kong by Dai Nippon Limited

First U.S. edition 1983
published by Van Nostrand Reinhold Company Inc.,
135 West 50th Street, New York, NY 10020

Designed and produced by the Rainbird Publishing Group Limited
40 Park Street, London W1Y 4DE

To William Mackintosh

NOTE: In order to comply with international regulations on reproducing stamps
most of the stamps are not reproduced actual size. For example: 66% denotes
$\frac{2}{3}$ actual size; 150% denotes $1\frac{1}{2}$ times actual size.

Contents

What are stamps?
1 The story of the posts 6
2 The birth of adhesive stamps 8
3 Definitive stamps of the world 10
4 Commemorative and special issues 14
5 Charity and semi-postal stamps 20
6 Booklets, coils, miniature sheets and composite stamps 24
7 Postal stationery 26
8 Airmails 28
9 Stamps for special purposes 32

How to collect stamps
10 Beginning a stamp collection 38
11 Albums and accessories 40
12 The anatomy of a stamp 42
13 Printing processes 44
14 General collecting 48
15 Thematic collecting 50
16 Postal history 54
17 Cinderella philately 58
18 Specialized philately 64
19 Arranging and writing up a collection 66

Organized philately
20 The beginning of philately 68
21 Stamp dealing and exhibiting 70
22 Reading about stamps 74

Identification of stamps by their inscription 76
Glossary of philatelic terms 78
Acknowledgments and Index 80

1 The story of the posts

Stamp collecting, or philately, is all about stamps – those brightly coloured bits of paper that adorn our mail. Adhesive postage stamps have been around for less than a century and a half but the postal services, of which they are an outward symbol, go back much farther in time. Before 1840, when adhesive stamps were adopted in Britain, there were handstruck stamps bearing the name of the place of posting and sometimes the date as well, but the amount of the postage was usually indicated in writing – in red to denote that it had been paid by the sender, or in black to show that it had to be collected from the recipient. The amount of postage depended largely on how far the letter travelled. Weight was secondary in importance to the number of sheets of paper comprising the letter, two sheets meaning double postage, three sheets treble and so on.

A public postal service was established in Britain in the mid-seventeenth century and placed on a proper footing after the Restoration of Charles II. The Postmaster General, Colonel Henry Bishop, was responsible for the introduction of the circular date mark which is known by his name to this day. In 1661 he announced, 'A stamp is invented that is putt upon every letter showing the date of the moneth that every letter comes to this office, so that no letter Carryer may dare to detayne a letter from post to post; which before was usual.' For centuries a 'stamp' meant the mark on a letter and although England had the first datestamps as such, other countries had undated marks on their mail at an even earlier time. Embossed, handstruck or hand-written marks were applied to letters by the officials of many postal services in Europe from the fourteenth century onwards.

Letters written on paper do not date back much before the thirteenth century, but long after that period letters were written on other materials, such as parchment and other kinds of animal skins. In Russia birch bark was extensively used. Most of these medieval letters were carried by private messengers, though numerous bodies organized quite sophisticated postal systems. The universities, for example, developed a network of posts across Europe in the Middle Ages, and the great monastic orders had their own postal service. Many of the merchant guilds operated posts for their members, not only within their own country but with similar groups of businessmen in other countries. These letters can often be identified by their wax seals, endorsements on the address side and, of course, the contents of the letters themselves. Kings and their courtiers had elaborate networks of post relays, using men mounted on swift horses to bear the royal dispatches from the court to the farthest parts of the kingdom. This was the theory at least, but in practice such relay systems

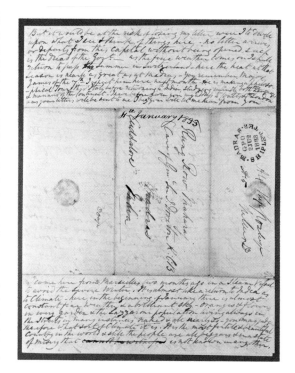

Typical of the letters before the advent of adhesive stamps. Note that the letter and its outer wrapper comprise a single sheet. The Madras Ship Letter mark denotes conveyance by private ship

were used mainly in time of war and at other periods were allowed to lapse. In Britain, for example, the earliest postal systems, dating from Tudor times, ran from London to Holyhead and thence to Ireland; from London to Dover and thence to the Continent; and from London to Berwick and thence to Scotland. These services were not available to the general public until about 1635, but thereafter it was increasingly possible for ordinary people to make use of the system and then the General Letter Office (later to become the General Post Office) was established in 1660.

From the outset the General Letter Office was clearly under government control and the right of transmitting letters continued to be a royal monopoly, just as it had been in the days when the Royal Mail literally meant that and no more. Similar systems of a government postal monopoly developed in most other countries although, as we shall see, an element of private enterprise was permitted in some parts of the world where the government posts could not or would not offer the full facilities.

Postal systems in the ancient world

But even farther back in time than the court, university, monastic and merchant posts of the Middle Ages there were postal services of a sort. A postal service was a mark of the level of literacy attained by any civilization and was a measure of the degree to which its administration was developed. The earliest references to a postal system are to be found in the Bible, in the books of Nehemiah and Esther, but we have actual evidence of posts from the large accumulation of clay tablets found at such sites as Tell el-Amarna in Egypt and Cappadocia in Turkey. And the Assyrian merchants of 3000 BC corresponded with their colleagues in many parts of western Asia by means of clay tablets written in the curious wedge-shaped script known as cuneiform writing. These tablets provide us with ample proof that elaborate systems of couriers existed five thousand years ago.

Historians credit King Cyrus of Persia with the creation of the first postal relay system, organized on modern lines. Rapid communications were a vital necessity to such a vast empire. The Greek city states had their own postal systems and these were later taken over by the Romans who developed a great network of good roads, from Exeter in the west to Edessa in the east, and established a regular system of posthouses and relay stations. The prefect of the Praetorian Guard administered the *Cursus Publicus* and was therefore the earliest postmaster general. Under him were the *curiosi*, or postal inspectors who supervised the *stationarii* (postmasters) and the *tabellarii* (letter carriers). This efficient system disappeared when the Roman Empire went into decline in the fifth century AD and a thousand years passed before

below **Cuneiform clay tablet,** *c.* **3000** BC

far below **Early nineteenth-century print showing the departure of the mailcoaches from the General Post Office in London**

anything like it re-emerged on a national scale.

Even after most European countries had organized a postal service within their boundaries it was exceedingly difficult to send a letter from one country to another. The postal charges could only be prepaid by the sender as far as the frontier, while the addressee had to pay the charges accruing between the frontier and the destination of the letter. Obviously in cases where letters had to be sent across other countries *en route* the system for computing the total charges due was much more complicated. Eventually reciprocal arrangements, known as postal treaties, were drawn up between various countries to facilitate the handling of international mail, but so long as each country had a cumbersome method of computing postage international mail was severely hampered.

Cheap postage and the UPU

After the Napoleonic Wars Europe entered a period of comparative tranquillity that greatly encouraged the development of trade and commerce. Rising standards of literacy and greater mobility of population encouraged letter writing, but charges were excessive. Everywhere the public clamoured for cheap postage. Britain led the way in the matter of postal reform, introducing Uniform Penny Postage in 1840, together with adhesive stamps which made the system much more convenient. Other countries followed suit: by 1860 the system of cheap postage, calculated by the weight of the letter, was well established. Montgomery Blair, the American Postmaster General, led the fight for greater international co-operation but he was prevented from putting his ideas into practice by the Civil War. In the end it was left to the Postmaster General of Prussia, Heinrich von Stephan, who used the expertise he had gained in welding together the numerous postal services of the German kingdoms and principalities when the German Empire was founded in 1871, to organize the General Postal Union (later to become the Universal Postal Union) in 1874. The UPU, with its headquarters in Berne, Switzerland, co-ordinates and administers international postal services with its highly complex accounting system. Virtually every country and postal administration now belongs to the UPU and it is this that permits the stamps of one country to be accepted for the prepayment of postage to every other member country without any surcharge raised at the destination and the UPU has continued to function smoothly throughout world wars and major political upheavals.

Such is the speed of modern postal communications that it is now possible to send a letter to the far side of the globe, and receive a reply, all within the space of a week. Where it once took three months to send a letter by sailing ship from England to Australia it now takes three days – and all due to an efficient international system that we tend to take for granted.

2 The birth of adhesive stamps

The plan for postal reform advocated by the Englishman Rowland Hill, a schoolmaster from Kidderminster, envisaged a drastic simplification of the method of calculating the postage and encouraging letter writers to pay the money in advance. Hitherto prepaid letters were relatively uncommon; it was not quite 'the done thing' for the sender to pay the postage! Nevertheless prepaid letters, mainly business correspondence, did exist before 1840 and the fact that the postage had been paid was denoted by handstruck 'stamps'. As early as 1680 William Dockwra organized a penny post in London and postmarks inscribed 'Penny post paid' were used. The government suppressed this piece of private enterprise within two years, but continued to operate it as part of the general postal service and, in fact, even used similar postmarks. Prepayment of postage by the sender in cash was sometimes indicated by striking the office postmark in red ink, the amount of postage being shown in red crayon: this practice has continued up to the present day in the guise of those red postmarks you often find on circulars. Apart from the official Post Office stamps there are meter marks, applied by business firms and other bodies, and these are likewise found, for the most part, in red ink. Even meter franking has, to some extent, been superseded by permit mailing and the use of postage-paid impressions, printed on envelopes and wrappers under a bulk-posting arrangement with the Post Office. But despite the widespread use of cash prepayment, meter franking and bulk posting, the public still find that adhesive stamps are the most convenient means of paying for their correspondence.

When Rowland Hill published his plan for Uniform Postage in 1839 he mentioned 'Slips of paper just large enough to bear the stamp . . . affixed to the letter by means of a glutinous wash'. This was something of an afterthought, since he pinned his faith mainly on elaborately designed envelopes and wrappers printed in black (one penny) or blue (two pence). The British public derided the pompous symbolism of these pictorial envelopes, produced by William Mulready, RA, and they were ignominiously withdrawn after a few months and replaced by envelopes and letter sheets with embossed stamps. This type of pre-printed postal stationery continues to the present day, but has always been less popular than adhesive stamps which can be affixed to any envelope, postcard or wrapper.

The invention of the adhesive stamp

The advent of the Penny Black and Twopence Blue in May 1840 revolutionized world communications and the repercussions are felt to this day. Inevitably other claimants have been put forward as the true inventors of the adhesive stamp. It should be noted that the idea of adhesive stamps was not novel in 1840, since various taxes had been paid by this method since the beginning of the nineteenth century. The size and format of the world's first adhesive postage stamps were derived from the gummed labels used to secure embossed tax stamps to legal documents. These labels even bore corner letters and die numbers – features that were to appear in the early British postage stamps. Nor was the principle of prepayment of postage by means of stamps (albeit handstruck ones) unknown in 1840. What was new, however, was the combination of prepayment with the idea of using adhesive labels.

Even this idea may well not be quite as innovatory as we think. In 1653 Renouard de Villayer

left **Portrait of Sir Rowland Hill, originator of the Penny Postage, by J. A. Vinter**

Mulready envelope bearing a Maltese Cross obliteration, the rare framed postmark of Barras Bridge receiving house – equivalent of the modern sub-post office

POSTAGE ONE PENNY.

organized a postal service in Paris known as the *Petit Poste* which made use of *billets de port payé* (tickets of postal payment), purchased for one sou. These *billets* were slips of printed paper affixed to letters by means of isinglass wafers. The sender did not need to take the letter to the post office, since postboxes were erected conveniently at street corners for this purpose. Unfortunately the scheme foundered because the postboxes were vandalized. Although this system is well documented in contemporary writings no example of a letter thus transmitted, or any of the *billets* themselves, have yet come to light.

In 1818 the postal administration of the kingdom of Sardinia introduced a stamped letter sheet, the *Carta postale bollata*, to be sold at all post offices. The use of these sheets was compulsory, and since the whole idea was to give the government rigid control of postal communication it has been argued that the stamps printed on these sheets were fiscal rather than postal. This seems to be mere hair-splitting and the Italians have always claimed, with some measure of justification, that they invented postal stationery. Three different stamps were printed on these sheets, all of them having as their motif a tiny picture of a postboy on a galloping horse, hence their nickname of *Cavallini* (little horsemen). The 15-centesimi stamp was circular and prepaid postage on a letter going 15 miles (24 km), the 25-centesimi stamp was oval (15 to 35 miles; 24 to 56 km) and the 50-centesimi stamp was octagonal (distances beyond 35 miles). The *Cavallini* were in use until 1836, on mail all over the kingdom of Sardinia, which included Piedmont and Savoy on the Italian mainland. A similar idea was proposed in Sweden (*Carta sigillata*, 'sealed sheets') but not adopted for postal purposes, though it was later used for legal documents. In 1838 the colonial authorities in New South Wales introduced letter sheets and wrappers for use on mail in and around Sydney. The postage was indicated by means of the colonial seal embossed in colourless relief. They were not very popular with the people of Sydney and though they were not superseded by adhesive stamps till 1850, used examples are quite scarce. Even after the birth of the Penny Black several countries preferred postal stationery and did not adopt adhesive stamps till some time later. Württemberg, Finland, Russia and Poland all had stamped envelopes and wrappers before they introduced adhesives.

Other claimants

Independently of Rowland Hill several men had the same bright idea. James Chalmers, a Dundee bookseller, took a keen interest in postal reform in the 1830s and is said to have produced his first essays in adhesive stamps as early as 1834, though this has since been hotly disputed and led to an astonishing feud between the Chalmers and Hill families that continues to this day! In 1836

L. Koschier, or Kŏsir, an Austrian civil servant in Laibach (modern Ljubljana in Yugoslavia) put forward a plan for adhesive stamps which was turned down by his superiors. Both Austria and Yugoslavia, however, now claim him as 'ideological creator' of the postage stamp – and have issued stamps in his honour. Oddly enough, the nearest actual contender for the title of the world's first stamp also comes from Austria. Shortly before the Second World War a letter discovered in an old book was found to bear a brown label inscribed *Franco* (i.e. post paid) with a numeral 1. The father of the letter writer was postmaster of Spital and it seems that he had hit upon this method of indicating that he had received the price of the postage. An Austrian philatelic commission was convened in 1952 and solemnly pronounced the Spital stamp to be genuine. Since it was an unofficial production, however, its status has not yet been recognized by the world's stamp catalogues.

The Queen's head

The advent of adhesive stamps in Britain was heralded by a competition, organized by the Treasury, in 1839. More than 2,600 entries were received but the vast majority envisaged some kind of postal stationery and only 45 suggested adhesive labels. Though prizes were awarded to four of the entries none of them was actually used. In the end it was Rowland Hill's own suggestion that was adopted. He felt that a device portraying the young Queen Victoria would not only be appropriate but would be very difficult to counterfeit, since the slightest alteration in the royal features would be readily detected. The profile of the Queen was based on William Wyon's Guildhall medal of 1838. Henry Corbould produced sketches of the profile, from which the engravers Charles and Frederick Heath produced the master die for the stamps. This portrait of Victoria as a teenager continued to grace all British stamps till 1902 – a year after the Queen died at the age of 83.

above **The 50-centesimi 'Cavallini' stamp from a Sardinian letter of 1820** (same size)

right **Obverse of the Guildhall medal sculpted by William Wyon, RA, showing the youthful Queen Victoria – model for all Victorian British stamps** (modern facsimile)

3 Definitive stamps of the world

In 1840 there was only one kind of adhesive postage stamp, comprising two values. The Penny Black prepaid postage on a ½-ounce (14 g) letter to any part of the United Kingdom; the Twopence Blue prepaid a 1-ounce (28 g) letter. Heavier letters were prepaid by means of pairs, blocks or strips of these stamps to the required sum. Letters could be registered, but prepayment was denoted by an endorsement in red ink and stamps were not, at first, used for this purpose. Because the colour made it difficult to see the cancellation the Penny Black was replaced by

the Penny Red in February 1841. In the few months of its existence, however, the Penny Black rapidly found favour with the public and over 70 million of them were printed. Quite a good proportion of these stamps seems to have survived and contrary to a widely held belief it is not a rare stamp. As the world's *first*, however, it is a stamp every collector would like to possess, and it is the astronomical global demand that has boosted its value to its present height. In various forms the Penny Red remained in use for 40 years and countless millions were used. Perforations were introduced in the 1850s and security letters subsequently inserted in the upper as well as the lower corners. Tiny numerals engraved in the side panels were another feature, in the 1860s, and indicated the plate from which the stamps had been printed. Eventually these plate numbers extended as high as 225. Very few stamps from Plate 77 were issued and these are now worth several thousand pounds apiece, but even a set of stamps representing each of the other plates would cost quite a lot of money to

put together. The design of the Twopence Blue was altered slightly in 1841 by the addition of horizontal white lines and thereafter underwent the same changes as the penny stamp till 1880 when it, too, was withdrawn.

The earliest British stamps are known to collectors as line-engraveds, from the method by which they were printed (see Printing Processes, p. 44). No additions to this series were made until 1870 when a tiny halfpenny stamp and a normal-sized 1½d stamp were introduced, both printed in the same shade of reddish brown as the penny stamp. Line engraving and recess printing were costly processes and they were discontinued in Britain in 1880. Long before that time, however, other processes had been tried for the higher denominations. Embossed stamps (like those printed on postal stationery) were introduced in 1847 following an Anglo-French postal treaty which meant that British stamps could prepay postage beyond the United Kingdom. The embossed stamps – sixpence purple, tenpence brown and shilling green – were imperforate like the line-engraveds, but being printed by hand, one at a time, often overlapped and were therefore difficult to cut apart: hence the comparative scarcity of nice, four-margined examples. In 1853 De La Rue began printing revenue stamps using the letterpress method and the following year they were given the contract to produce 4d stamps by this process. Gradually De La Rue took over printing all the stamps from 3d to £5 by this method and in 1880 even the ½d–2d stamps.

The idea spreads from Britain

Adhesive stamps spread slowly to other countries. An Englishman, Henry T. Windsor, operated the New York City Dispatch Post and in 1842 introduced adhesive stamps portraying George Washington. The following year adhesive stamps appeared in Brazil and came to be known as the 'Bullseyes' on account of their unusual numeral design. Shortly afterwards the Swiss cantons of Zürich and Geneva began issuing stamps with numeral and heraldic motifs respectively. The Geneva stamp was something of a curiosity since it consisted of two 5-cent stamps joined to form one 10-cent stamp: hence its nickname, the 'Double Geneva'. In 1845 the canton of Basle joined in, with its famous 'Dove' design. This was the first stamp to be printed in a country other than the one that issued it, having been printed at Frankfurt-am-Main in Germany. It was also the first stamp to be printed by two different processes (letterpress and embossing); and it was bicoloured, following the practice of Zürich and Geneva, which had also dabbled in two-colour printing. In 1847 the postmaster of New York issued a handsome black stamp – again portraying Washington – and in the same

left **The Twopence Blue of 1840** (379%)

above **The Penny Black** (155%)

year the first British colony, Mauritius, issued 1d and 2d stamps crudely modelled on the contemporary British issues. The famous Mauritius 'Post Office' stamps were actually preceded by Trinidad's 'Lady McLeod' stamp, but as the latter was a private issue by a coastal shipping company the Mauritius pair rank as the first official British colonials.

Bermuda's circular stamps, produced by postmaster William Perot, appeared in 1848 and the following year stamps were introduced by Bavaria, Belgium and France. Australia's first adhesives, the celebrated 'Sydney Views', appeared in 1850 and Asia's first stamps, the embossed Scinde (Sind) 'Dawks', appeared two years later. Thereafter stamps spread like wildfire and by the end of the 1850s most of the principal countries of the world had adopted these small scraps of gummed paper which were revolutionizing the handling and accounting of mail.

Postal conventions

Long before the Universal Postal Union, postal treaties and conventions were arranged between groups of countries. The most important of these was the German-Austrian postal convention of 1850 which not only facilitated the free passage of mail among the various kingdoms and principalities in Germany, Austria and northern Italy (then under Austrian rule), but played an important part in influencing the colours used for the various postal rates. This was a principle that the Universal Postal Union tried to develop, but it was not until 1891 that a colour code was agreed. Henceforward green was reserved for the printed matter and inland postcard rates, red for the inland letter and overseas postcard rates, and blue for the overseas letter rate. At the turn of the century, therefore, these colours were widely used in the British Empire for the ½d, 1d and 2½d stamps respectively, and had their counterparts in many other countries. Thus green was the colour of the American 1 cent, the French 5 centimes and the German 5 pfennig, red the colour of the 2 cents, 10 centimes and 10 pfennig, and blue the colour of the 5 cents, 25 centimes and 25 pfennig. The UPU colour code continued until the First World War when inflation played havoc with postal charges, but it lingered on in Britain till the Second World War, and in the United States till the 1950s.

The earliest stamps were of purely local validity and for that reason there was no need to include the name of the issuing country in the inscription. In practice, however, many nations included some reference to the country of issue, especially from 1850 onwards when the number of different stamps was rising rapidly. Britain clung to the tradition that Queen Victoria's profile was sufficient identification and when the Universal Postal Union in 1874 stipulated that all stamps must bear the country name, Britain was exempted in view of her position as the premier stamp issuer. This custom has continued

United States definitive of 1963 without a country name (107%)

right down to the present day and was no mere conceit since no inscription would have adequately expressed the area in which the stamps were valid. Such expressions as 'Great Britain' or 'United Kingdom' would have been incorrect, since British stamps were also used in the Channel Islands and the Isle of Man which, constitutionally speaking, are not part of the United Kingdom. Since 1969 Guernsey and Jersey have issued their own stamps, and the Isle of Man followed suit in 1973, so it would now be possible to use a term such as 'UK Posts' but the tradition of anonymity has lasted for 140 years and is unlikely to be dropped. From time to time, of course, other countries have breached the UPU regulation and as recently as 1963 the United States issued stamps depicting the Stars and Stripes over the White House without an indication of the country of origin. Doubtless it was felt that 'Old Glory' was sufficient identification! By and large, however, the regulation is closely adhered to, even if the inscription is sometimes obscure or cryptical.

The definitives

Nowadays the term definitive is widely used to denote those stamps that are the maids of all work in a country's postal service. They are the permanent series forming the backbone of postal requirements. In Britain, for example, the great majority of the definitives have been remarkably uniform in concept. With the exception of the highest denominations and the halfpenny of 1870–80, they have followed the upright format adopted in 1840. They have all portrayed the reigning monarch. From time to time there may have been attempts to inject greater artistry into the designs – usually resulting in rather fussy heraldic or symbolic ornament – but pictorialism was rigidly excluded on the grounds that it was impossible to do adequate justice to the pictures. The only concession by the Post Office, after a sustained campaign by philatelists and the general public for more attractive stamps, was the issue of four high values in 1951 with scenic vignettes on the 2s 6d and 5s and heraldry on the 10s and £1 followed by the Castles high values of 1954–68. The double-sized high values of the reign of George V are known as the 'Seahorses' from their symbolic element, but these cannot be regarded as pictorial in the true sense.

Other countries at first adopted a similar approach, but even from the 1840s there were several schools of thought regarding the subjects to be depicted on the stamps. Portraits of reigning monarchs were not as popular as might have been expected. Brazil balked at portraying Dom Pedro II and used numeral motifs instead. Spain and Naples used portraits of their rulers, but went to great lengths to devise elaborate cancellations that would frame the royal features without disfiguring them. Although every country in Europe (except France and Switzerland) had a monarchy in the mid-nineteenth century, only Portugal, Belgium, the Netherlands and Luxemburg adopted royal portraiture from the beginning. Other countries used numeral designs (notably the Scandinavian group) or heraldry, while the republics used mythological or allegorical figures: Ceres (France) and Helvetia (Switzerland). Later on, the imperial profile of Napoleon III was substituted when the Second Empire was proclaimed, but after the débâcle of 1870–1 republican allegory was revived in the guise of Ceres, Marianne, La Semeuse and now the Sabine Women. Austria and a few of the German states, including Prussia, subsequently used royal portraits, but the German Empire preferred armorial or allegorical designs. The Wagnerian figure of Germania was adopted in 1900 and for all his vanity, Kaiser Wilhelm II had to be content with a tiny portrait amid the crowd scenes depicted on the higher values.

The United States was the most enthusiastic follower of the portrait tradition but banned the portrayal of living persons. Instead the pantheon of former (and long-dead) presidents and heroes of the War of Independence provided a seemingly inexhaustible supply of subjects. The only divergence from this policy was the very handsome series of 1869 with its tiny pictorial motifs, and a few of the denominations in the definitives of the 1920s and early 1930s, but this was followed by the series of 1938 which portrayed every president from Washington (1 cent) to Calvin Coolidge ($5). To encourage Americans to memorize the number of their presidents each number up to the 22nd president (Grover Cleveland) was represented by a denomination of the same value in cents. The dates of each presidential term were also included in the inscription. The problem of fractional denominations was

met by depicting other subjects: Benjamin Franklin ($\frac{1}{2}$ cent), Martha Washington ($1\frac{1}{2}$ cents) and the White House ($4\frac{1}{2}$ cents). The definitives since 1954, while continuing the presidential theme, have widened their scope to include eminent Americans in other fields, plus a measure of symbolism and historic landmarks. More recent definitive sets, of 1965 and 1970, were devoted entirely to prominent Americans, whereas the series in progress since 1975, strongly influenced by the bicentennial celebrations, has been inspired by the revolutionary period.

Latin American countries have tended to follow the United States with a mixture of presidential portraiture and republican allegory. A more frankly pictorial approach was adopted, however, at the turn of the century as a result of the activities of Nicholas Seebeck, an entrepreneur who persuaded a number of countries to change their definitives every year, on condition that he was allowed to reprint the stamps for his own purposes. The prolific issues that then ensued have resulted in the so-called 'Seebeck' countries lingering under a cloud to this day.

Until the Second World War the British Empire accounted for more than half the world's output of stamps. The great majority of colonial stamps followed the mother country in portraying the monarch and this led to the increasing use of colonial keyplates of identical designs, only the name of the colony and the value being altered. Keyplates were also extensively used by the other colonial powers in their respective territories. Thus the German colonies had stamps showing the Kaiser's yacht *Hohenzollern*; French colonies had allegorical figures representing Peace, Commerce and Navigation; Spanish territories traced the development of

A range of stamps used by the Australian states, prior to the introduction of the Commonwealth issues in 1913. *Top row:* **New South Wales, including two of the earliest commemorative stamps;** *middle row:* **Queensland and South Australia;** *bottom row:* **Van Diemen's Land (Tasmania), Victoria and Western Australia** (actual size)

Alfonso XIII from infancy to manhood in the famous 'Baby' and 'Curlyhead' issues; and the Portuguese colonies used royal portraits and then republican allegory.

Pictorial and armorial definitives

Apart from the short-lived American series of 1869 the first real break with portraiture and allegory came at the end of the nineteenth century. New South Wales celebrated its centenary in 1888 with a series of charming pictorial designs. Though intended primarily as a commemorative series this set was retained on a permanent basis for more than a decade. New Zealand launched a more ambitious pictorial series in 1898, dwelling heavily on the scenic beauties of that country. Newfoundland mixed pictorial designs with portraiture (including lesser members of the Royal Family) and this dual system was to continue until 1949 when it joined the Canadian confederation. Canada itself had alternated between royal portraits and pictorialism from the early years of this century and this blend continues to this day. Even the smaller colonies and protectorates abandoned

the keyplate system in the 1920s and 1930s and turned increasingly to pictorial designs, often in attractive two-colour combinations, and a similar policy was adopted by the other colonial powers in the same period. By this time the revenue from sales to collectors was becoming more important.

The smaller countries of Europe also appreciated the advantages of pictorial designs and it is significant that the most attractive stamps in the period prior to the Second World War came from Andorra, Monaco, San Marino and Liechtenstein. Though continuing to use republican allegory for the lower denominations France began using double-sized scenic pictorials for the higher values in 1929 and this practice has continued until the present day. A third element, consisting of multicoloured stamps featuring coats of arms, was introduced in 1946 and is used mainly for the very lowest denominations. The French system of blending small-format allegorical designs with large-format pictorials has since been extended to other countries.

Today the most conservative countries are the Scandinavian group whose definitives include a high proportion of royal-portrait stamps, allegorical and numerical designs and, apart from Sweden, little emphasis is laid on pictorial designs. Denmark's current high values perpetuate a design introduced in 1946, but Norway holds the world record for longevity, with the posthorn and numeral design which was first used more than a century ago and is still going strong! During that period, of course, it has undergone numerous changes in value, colour and printing process. Other countries with long-service records include the Sudan, whose Camel Postman design was used from 1898 till 1951 (and on the top values since then), the Irish Republic (1922–68), and Tonga (1897–1953).

In most countries, however, the definitive series changes every few years, ten years being a good average, though most of the remaining colonial territories change every five, and some Third World countries adopt new designs every other year.

right **Cover commemorating the Royal Visit of King George VI and Queen Elizabeth to Canada in 1939; it bears the special cancellation of the Royal Train**

below left **The present trend is towards larger and more colourful definitives with completely pictorial motifs, with the emphasis on fauna, flora, scenery and other popular themes** (actual size)

below right **Pictorial definitive stamps, showing that quite an attractive picture can be reproduced in a limited space. Prewar stamps of Tunisia and Czechoslovakia, contrasted with modern stamps from Austria, Czechoslovakia, West Germany and Yugoslavia** (actual size)

4 Commemorative and special issues

A commemorative stamp is one that is issued to mark a historic anniversary or personality, or to publicize a current event. The topical nature of such issues means that they are usually of short duration, compared with the definitives which are more permanent. In recent years the criteria governing commemoratives have tended to become rather blurred. In many cases a historic event is little more than a peg on which to hang an issue, and the stamps may consequently have little relevance to the event celebrated. The Wild Birds series issued by Britain in the spring of 1980 is a good example of this. Ostensibly they commemorate the centenary of the Wild Birds Protection Act, but no mention of this appears on the stamps. This and other borderline cases are now designated as 'special issues' rather than as 'commemoratives', but they have one thing in common – they are generally on sale for a fairly short period. Other features possessed by many (though by no means all) commemoratives are their larger format, greater use of pictorialism and generally more eye-catching appearance – all calculated to attract the collector. The potential philatelic revenue often tempted postal administrations into issuing long and expensive sets, but nowadays a more moderate policy of 'little, but often' is pursued.

The idea that a postage stamp might have some ulterior motive than the prepayment of postage was slow to develop. Although some philatelists claim that the stamps issued by Baden in 1851 should be classed as commemoratives, because they bear tiny inscriptions in the side panels commemorating the Austro-German Postal Treaty which led to their inception, this is usually dismissed as purely incidental. Similarly the British definitives that made their début in 1887 did *not* commemorate Queen Victoria's Golden Jubilee, even though they are commonly known as the Jubilee series.

Until recently it was fashionable to give the Australian state of New South Wales credit for the world's first commemorative stamps in the true sense: the series captioned 'One Hundred Years', issued in 1888 to celebrate the centenary of the British settlement. Opinion has now shifted in favour of Peru which issued a 5-centavos stamp in 1871, showing a railway train above the national coat of arms. The borders of the design were inscribed 'Chorillos–Lima–Callao' and it is only within recent years that the significance of this has been realized. The names are those of the main points on the Peruvian railway which was opened in 1851. Thus this stamp is regarded as commemorating the 20th anniversary of the railway. Normally a feature of commemorative stamps is a date or dates, and this is absent from the Peruvian stamp and it is perhaps significant that this interesting precedent was not followed

up until 1897 when a set of three bearing that date prominently celebrated the opening of the new postal headquarters in Lima. The New South Wales stamps, on the other hand, were clearly and unequivocally captioned to indicate their purpose, and the top value of the series even went so far as to portray the governors in 1788 and 1888 – Arthur Phillip and Lord Carrington – with their respective dates. (In the same year New South Wales issued postal stationery with a commemorative inscription to celebrate the 50th anniversary of the embossed stationery of 1838,

Modern commemorative and special issues rely heavily on large formats and multi-colour printing to achieve startling effects (106%)

but this was not so innovative since the United States had celebrated the centenary of the Declaration of Independence with specially embossed stationery in 1876.) Even the series of 1888 could only claim to be the first government-issued commemorative set, since a private postal service in Germany had previously issued stamps in honour of a local shooting competition.

The next country to issue commemoratives was Hong Kong, which celebrated the golden jubilee of the British settlement by re-issuing the 2 cents definitive with an appropriate overprint flanked by the dates 1841 and 1891. This was not only Asia's first commemorative but the first to make use of a practice that has since become widespread: the conversion of one stamp into another by means of an overprint. Such a subterfuge is seldom popular with collectors who feel cheated that any postal administration should resort to such a cheap method of celebrating events which would be worthy of more distinctive issues. This ruse was adopted by the tiny Balkan kingdom of Montenegro in 1893 when seven of the definitive stamps were overprinted for the rather esoteric purpose of celebrating the quatercentenary of printing in Montenegro. Three years later, however, the Njegoš dynasty celebrated its bicentenary and Montenegro dutifully recorded the occasion with a dozen stamps depicting the monastery at 'commemoratives', but they have one thing in prominently celebrated the opening of the new Cetinje. For years the mint set was a drug on the market but used copies are worth rather more.

Commemoratives as revenue earners

The first of the long and extremely expensive commemorative sets, which were to incur the wrath of contemporary collectors, was released by the United States in 1893 to publicize the Columbian Exposition which, in turn, celebrated the quatercentenary of the discovery of America by Columbus. This handsome series, mainly reproducing paintings illustrating the career of Columbus, ranged from 1 cent up to $5, and a novel feature of the top value was that it featured the coin issued to commemorate the same event. Other countries in the Western Hemisphere also issued stamps in honour of Columbus and by the end of the century he was reputed to have appeared on more stamps than

anyone else – other than Queen Victoria!

The first commemorative stamp from Africa was a penny stamp issued by the Transvaal in 1895, appropriately celebrating the introduction of penny postage. Apart from Montenegro the earliest European commemoratives came from San Marino, which issued four stamps in 1894 to mark the installation of the new regents. As the two regents or presidents were elected half-yearly this precedent might have resulted in new commemoratives every six months but mercifully no attempt was made to follow it up. Though San Marino later acquired an unenviable reputation for churning out new stamps it did not issue another commemorative set until 1918, to celebrate the Italian victory over Austria.

The commemorative stamp came to be associated with small and impecunious countries, which were quick to appreciate the tremendous revenues to be gained from collectors. It is significant that the more important European countries ignored this medium or were slow to adopt it. Though the private posts of Germany made use of commemoratives from time to time, and both Bavaria and Württemberg had commemorative sets, in 1911 and 1916 respectively, Germany itself did not issue such stamps till 1919. France's first commemorative was an overprinted issue for a stamp exhibition in 1923, followed by the Olympic Games set of 1924, and in the same year Britain issued two stamps for the British Empire Exhibition at Wembley. The upheavals of the First World War gave commemorative stamps their greatest stimulus up to that time and included sets from Bulgaria and Turkey which had been prepared in anticipation of military conquests that did not materialize. Nearer the present day Togo issued a set commemorating a summit conference which was called off by Russia at the last moment!

From the outset commemorative stamps were regarded as a mixed blessing. Even the issuing countries tended to limit their validity to internal mail, or made complex arrangements with their immediate neighbours to accept mail franked by these stamps. Had commemoratives been confined to single stamps of low denomination they might have become more acceptable, but there was a marked tendency in the 1890s and early 1900s to issue long sets with a very high face value. The worst offenders in this respect were the United States, a number of the Latin American republics and Canada, the last-named producing a set from $\frac{1}{2}$ cent to $5 in honour of Queen Victoria's Diamond Jubilee in 1897. A similarly lengthy set, but more modestly priced and with much greater variety in its designs, was produced for the same event by Newfoundland. The Diamond Jubilee, in fact, triggered off commemorative issues from no fewer than eight British overseas territories, though it was ignored by the British Post Office. Portugal was another excessive issuer of commemoratives, its long historical sets appearing at virtually annual

The world's first commemoratives: New South Wales, 1888 (Australia); Hong Kong Jubilee, 1891 (Asia); Columbus quatercentenary, 1893 (America); Montenegro printing quatercentenary, 1894 (Europe); Transvaal Penny Postage, 1895 (Africa); and the first omnibus series, the Vasco da Gama quatercentenary issue of 1898 (66%)

intervals from 1894. In 1898 a set of eight stamps was issued to celebrate the quatercentenary of Vasco da Gama's discovery of the sea route to India. This was released simultaneously in the overseas territories, with appropriate inscriptions and values in local currencies.

Omnibus issues

This practice of issuing stamps in a number of countries with uniform designs was fortunately slow to catch on. It was not repeated until 1931 when France issued stamps throughout its colonial empire in honour of the Colonial Exhibition in Paris. France repeated the exercise in 1937 to commemorate the Exposition Internationale in Paris and two years later produced a similar issue in honour of the New York World's Fair. Such series, known as omnibus issues, were a logical extension of the colonial keyplate system which had previously been used for definitives. Britain adopted this principle in 1935 with uniform sets of four stamps in each colony and protectorate to celebrate the Silver Jubilee of King George V, and two years later repeated the process with sets of three for the Coronation of King George VI. Thereafter France and Britain, and to a lesser extent Spain, Portugal, Belgium and the Netherlands, resorted to omnibus issues for their colonial empires. Even since 1958, when the old French colonial empire was replaced by the French Community, this principle has continued. The British colonies continued to issue omnibus sets of identical designs until the mid-1960s, when declining sales forced the Crown Agents to rethink their policy. As a result, omnibus issues since then have had an underlying theme and an overall concept, but the individual designs have been distinctive. The Silver Wedding series of 1972, for example, had uniform frames, incorporating portraits of the Queen and Duke of Edinburgh, but the central vignettes and secondary ornament varied from colony to colony. The Silver Jubilee series of 1977 consisted of three stamps from each territory, with subjects which, taken together, traced the story of the Coronation from start to finish. The Coronation Anniversary series the following year took as its theme the Queen's Beasts, the heraldic stone figures that lined the entrance to Westminster Abbey, and included local beasts rendered in the same sculptural fashion.

The loosening of old political ties means that the more independent members of the French Community or the Commonwealth tend to produce stamps in quite distinct designs, even when they participate in honouring a common event. Moreover, since the Second World War there has been a tendency for many countries, with no political affiliations, to issue stamps in commemoration of the same event, either because they have a common interest in the event, or more probably because they realize that that particular event has captured the attention of collectors. Far more countries, for example,

celebrated the end of the Second World War than commemorated the end of the First World War, and included lengthy omnibus issues from both British and French colonial empires. The 75th anniversary of the Universal Postal Union in 1949 was the first major international event to receive the full commemorative treatment from virtually every stamp-issuing country – an event exceeded only by the centenary itself in 1974.

Not only important international events, but personalities of world renown, have been honoured in this way. The assassination of John F. Kennedy in 1963 precipitated sets of mourning stamps from many countries. Little more than a year later the death of Winston Churchill resulted in a worldwide spate of stamps in his memory, including a lengthy colonial omnibus series of uniform design. The birth centenary of Churchill in 1974 provoked an even greater response, though this time the colonial issues were all distinctive.

Sports commemoratives

Perhaps the greatest opportunity for worldwide commemorative issues is sport, and this goes back to 1896 when Greece, as host of the first of the modern Olympic Games, produced a set of 12 stamps with classical sporting themes. An even longer series appeared in 1906 when Greece hosted the 'mid-term' Olympics, but it was not until 1920, when Belgium was the host country, that commemoratives honouring the Olympics appeared elsewhere. Thereafter sets were produced by the host country for every Summer Games and, since 1932, for the Winter Games as well. Uruguay celebrated the victory of its team in the Olympic football series at the 1924 Games with a set of three stamps, and repeated the process after victory in the 1928 Games, but the idea of Olympic stamps being issued by participants, as well as the hosts, did not gain ground till the 1950s. Since then, however, it has got out of hand and we now have the ludicrous situation of long and expensive sets from countries that

Omnibus issues for the Silver Jubilee, 1935; Victory, 1946; Coronation of King George VI, 1937; and the 75th Anniversary of the Universal Postal Union, 1949 (actual size)

Special issues with a
message: Spain (fire
prevention); Tanzania
(wildlife protection);
Ghana and Australia
(food production);
Ghana (blindness
prevention); Switzer-
land (wartime
salvage); Venezuela
and Italy ('pay your
taxes'); Argentina,
Netherlands and
United States
(postcodes and Zip
code); Rhodesia
(anti-pollution);
United States (family
planning); Turkey
(road safety); Guyana
(savings bonds); and
Italy (drug abuse).
(actual size)

have not the remotest intention of taking part in
the Games. Australia set an awkward, and
much-criticized, precedent in 1954 by issuing a
stamp as advance publicity for the Melbourne
Olympics of 1956. This ides has since been
copied by other host countries and the Soviet
Union began issuing stamps for the 1980
Olympics in 1977, producing well over a hundred
collectable items in the period before the Games
themselves. Even the United States issued stamps
for the Moscow Olympics nine months before
the event – an issue which was to cause intense
embarrassment to the Carter administration in
its subsequent attempts to boycott the Games.

There was a time when most countries used
commemoratives sparingly. In the period up to
the Second World War a country might issue
only one set in ten years, but would then provide
the full range of denominations from the lowest
to the highest value. This was frowned on by
collectors and dealers alike and attempts were

made to boycott these sets; but with the passage
of time they have become respectable and since
the demand far exceeds the supply they have
risen rapidly in value. Over the past forty years
there has been a tendency towards shorter sets
and even single stamps, but most countries now
produce commemoratives quite frequently. In
the period down to the end of the reign of George
VI Britain produced a dozen commemorative
issues; nowadays six or more sets are produced
each year. Also the number of stamps in each set
is slowly creeping up and, of course, the face value
has risen sharply as postal rates have increased.

Special issues

Another modern tendency is to issue short pictorial sets from time to time without the pretext
of an anniversary or current event. This policy
was adopted in Britain in the mid-1960s as a
means of catching up on the rest of the world
which had used the medium of commemoratives

to promote a national image or to educate people about a country's achievements. In 1966 alone three sets featured British landscapes, British birds and British technology, and have since been followed by sets devoted to flowers, trees, bridges, ships, architecture, explorers, medieval warriors, energy resources, horses, dogs and London landmarks. An immensely popular subject for special, non-commemorative issues has been paintings. The development of multi-colour printing processes in the 1950s encouraged France, Czechoslovakia and Hungary to issue handsome stamps reproducing famous paintings and other countries, including Britain, quickly followed suit. Since then other branches of the fine and applied arts have been explored and reproduced on stamps.

Special issues are also produced for seasonal occasions, such as Christmas, Easter and New Year (Christian, Jewish and Chinese versions). There have been sporadic issues for Mother's Day, and many countries now honour Stamp Day with an issue whose profits are used to subsidize stamp exhibitions. Some of the younger countries, a bit short on historic events to commemorate, have generated a wide range of annual events celebrated by stamps. In addition the United Nations now promotes occasions such as International Year of the Child or International Hydrological Decade, which provide ideal excuses for widespread issues of stamps. Many special issues are used for propaganda: warning against drug abuse, the hazards of forest fire and careless driving, or urging the populace to pay its taxes on time. Quite a collection could be formed of stamps encouraging one to use the postcode or its equivalent in countries that have introduced postal mechanization.

A further example of the trend towards the issue of stamps with uniform designs or themes in countries without any clearly defined political grouping, and sometimes no more than a common interest in the matter commemorated, is afforded by Norden ('The North'). This is the name given to the association of Scandinavian countries originally formed in 1919. On several occasions since 1956 Norden has issued stamps for Northern Countries Day. The first of these joint issues using virtually identical designs featured five swans in flight. Each of the participating countries – Denmark, Finland, Iceland, Norway and Sweden – issued two stamps in red (internal mail) and blue (external letters). Only the country names and the values differed. This interesting experiment was not repeated till 1969 when the golden jubilee of Norden was celebrated by an omnibus series with five Viking longships as its motif. Since then there has been a series (1977) depicting five waterlilies.

Europa and CEPT issues
The year 1956 also saw the start of another and more far-reaching omnibus series. Belgium, the Netherlands and Luxemburg, together with France, Germany and Italy, formed the European Coal and Steel Community, later developed into the European Economic Community and nicknamed the 'Common Market' or 'the Six'. As an outward sign of their unity they agreed to issue stamps each year with a common design.

The first issue took as its motif a scaffolded tower inscribed 'Europa'. After this demonstration of solidarity, however, each country went its own way in 1957 and produced its own interpretation of the 'Europa' theme, but in 1958 they managed to agree on a common design – a dove surmounting a letter E, and the following year six interlocking rings were used.

In 1960 the EEC surrendered the concept to the Conférence Européenne des Postes et Télécommunications (CEPT) which had been formed the previous year. This was a much wider union at a purely postal level and included Britain which issued Europa stamps in 1960 and 1961, but did not participate again until 1980. For a number of years the CEPT consisted of 19 member countries and this taxed the ingenuity of artists in designing symbolic motifs embodying 19 elements, the prize going to Pentti Rahikainen of Finland who designed the 1960 symbol – a wheel with 19 spokes. Later artists abandoned the numerical principle and settled for interlocking angles (1963), a stylized ship (1966), cogwheels (1967), a key (1968), a colonnade (1969), a flaming sun (1970), a chain (1971), an abstract symbolizing communications (1972) and a posthorn (1973).

Latterly it was felt that the common designs had become rather monotonous so the CEPT members decided to revert to the 1957 idea of individual interpretations of a common theme.

A selection of Christmas stamps from Malawi, Colombia, Samoa, Uruguay and Australia (actual size)

Since then the various subjects chosen have been sculptures (1974), paintings (1975), traditional crafts (1976), landmarks (1977), architecture (1978), postal and telecommunications history (1979) and famous persons (1980). As a result, the designs of Europa stamps in recent years have been extremely varied, the only common factors being the word 'Europa' and the CEPT emblem of interlocking posthorns. Europa stamps have been issued by most countries in western Europe, and, in the Mediterranean area, by Malta, Cyprus, Turkey and Yugoslavia.

Other joint issues

The Communist bloc has nothing comparable to the Europa series, though stamps with uniform designs have been issued by the eastern countries to mark the Warsaw Pact and Comecon, the Communist economic union. Mini-omnibus issues have also been made by the Benelux countries – and by Turkey, Iran and Pakistan which formed the Regional Development Co-operation Pact in 1964. The RDC stamps, as they are known, began with common symbolic motifs but latterly used designs derived from the applied and fine arts of the respective countries.

Joint issues using similar designs have been made on a number of occasions. Thus the United States cooperated with Canada in issuing virtually identical stamps for the opening of the St Lawrence Seaway in 1959 and the American Bicentennial in 1976 (the latter portraying Benjamin Franklin who had been Postmaster of British North America). The United States took part in joint issues with Mexico in 1960 and Spain in 1965. Britain, New Zealand and Australia made a joint issue in 1963 for the opening of the COMPAC cable, and the two Pacific countries issued identical stamps honouring Kingsford Smith (1958) and Winston Churchill (1965). Both Australia and New Zealand also produced a number of omnibus issues for their dependent territories in the 1950s and 1960s.

The ultimate in joint issues came in 1965 when Romania and Yugoslavia celebrated the opening of the Djerdap Dam with two stamps featuring the dam. The country names appeared in the vertical side panels and each stamp was inscribed 'Posta' with numerals of value in Romanian bani and Yugoslavian dinars. The stamps were released simultaneously in both countries. It is interesting to note that credit for the first simultaneous issue might have gone to France and Britain, which had planned a series commemorating the Anglo-French Entente in 1940. The stamps portrayed King George VI and the French president and bore values in centimes and pence. The occupation of France by Germany in the summer of 1940, however, prevented this set being issued.

Some of the many stamps issued by CEPT countries in honour of the Europa concept; the top row shows individual interpretations of the posthorn symbol adopted by all issuing countries in 1973. In more recent years a uniform theme has been chosen but the subject matter varies from country to country (118%)

5 Charity and semi-postal stamps

Stamp collectors are – albeit unintentionally – extremely charitable people who have at one time or another contributed large sums to such diverse good causes as TB sanatoria in Bulgaria, spastic clinics in Belgium, children's holiday camps in New Zealand and Fiji, and social welfare in the Netherlands. They have helped lepers in the Congo, unemployed intellectuals in France and refugees in India. They have provided milk for children in St Lucia and uniforms for the militia in Sweden. They have subsidized the rebuilding of churches (Gouda in the Netherlands and Orval Abbey in Belgium), helped to build hospitals for the blind (Egypt) and cancer patients (Norway), and succoured the victims of hurricanes in Samoa, earthquakes in Greece and Nicaragua, floods in the Netherlands and volcanic eruption in Indonesia. There is hardly a catastrophe, large or small, from a dam burst in France to an avalanche in Austria, that stamp collectors have not alleviated to some extent. How has this been done? The answer is the charity stamp, or semi-postal (to use the American term) since only part of the price of the stamp may be charged for postage and the rest goes to charity.

Charity stamps may be said to have had their origin in Britain which issued a pictorial envelope in 1890 to commemorate the golden jubilee of Penny Postage. Postally valid for one penny, it was actually sold for 1s, and the balance of 11d went to the Rowland Hill Benevolent Fund for postmen's widows and orphans. At the time of Queen Victoria's Diamond Jubilee in 1897 labels were produced for the Prince of Wales Hospital Fund but had no postal validity. This idea was, however, taken up by two of the Australian states, New South Wales and Victoria, each of which issued 1d and 2½d stamps to commemorate the Jubilee, but actually sold them at twelve times their face value (i.e. for 1s and 2s 6d respectively). Neither of the Victorian stamps mentions their charitable aspect, though the 2½d included an allegory of caring for the sick. The New South Wales stamps, however, were captioned 'Consumptives Home' in large lettering and showed the amount of postage as well as the total cost of each stamp. The dates of the Jubilee were relegated to a minor role. Victoria followed this with a pair of stamps in 1900, bearing large premiums in aid of Boer War charities.

This practice soon spread to Europe; both Russia and Romania were early adopting it on a regular basis. The outrageously high premiums of the early Australian stamps gave way to a more moderate policy, whereby the postage and charity premium were sometimes the same but more often the latter was much smaller. Nowadays the Fédération Internationale de Philatelie condemns any stamp that includes a premium amounting to more than 50 per cent of the face value, but this has not deterred some unscrupulous postal administrations from mulcting the collector as much as possible.

Charity stamps can generally be recognized by the fact that two values are quoted, linked by a plus sign. Occasionally the sums are clearly captioned 'Postage', 'Charity' or some similar word. An example of this is Britain's first (and so far only) charity stamp in which the expression of value – '4½ + 1½p for health and handicap charities' – took up half the area of the stamp!

Despite the promising start by New South Wales and Victoria, Australia has never had a charity stamp since it began issuing stamps in 1913. The United States is another country which has so far avoided this practice. Other countries, however, have issued charity stamps at frequent intervals and for all manner of good causes. Austria, Belgium, France, Switzerland and Romania were all at one time prolific producers of charity stamps and there was a period in Nazi Germany (1938–40) when virtually every issue bore an enormous premium (often several times the postal value) in aid of Hitler's Culture Fund. In more recent years, however, the practice of issuing charity stamps has lost ground very considerably and there have been many instances of stamps issued as part of a campaign to save the temples of Nubia or the art treasures of Florence which have not included a premium where one might have expected it. Instead the postal administrations usually arrange that a part of the philatelic revenue accruing from sales of these stamps is donated to charity.

Regular charity issues

Charity stamps can be divided into groups and some of these have a large following, despite the fact that their postal value is only a part of the price which has to be paid to acquire them. These are annual issues of long standing and it is possible to form specialized collections devoted entirely to them. First in this field are the children's charity stamps issued by Switzerland since 1913. Known to collectors as Pro Juventute (from their Latin inscription meaning 'on behalf of youth') they began modestly with a single stamp, but two stamps were released in 1915 and then three each year from 1916 till 1921. Thereafter four stamps were issued till 1947 when a fifth was added. The series reverted to four stamps in 1967 and continues at that level. Much of the appeal of the Pro Juventute stamps springs from their attractive subjects. Over the years such themes as cantonal coats of arms, costume, historic personalities, flowers, butterflies, birds, wildlife and fruits of the forest have been featured, the various subjects spreading over several years' issues in some cases.

Charity or semi-postal stamps include Swiss Pro Patria and Pro Juventute stamps, a Dutch children's stamp, Belgian and Philippines anti-TB stamps, and German welfare stamps. Britain's only charity issue appears bottom left (87 %)

Inspired by the success of the Pro Juventute stamps Switzerland began issuing annual stamps for the National Fête and adding a premium in aid of funds for Swiss expatriates, destitute mothers, the Red Cross, national defence, war relief, educational aid for invalids and the anti-cancer campaign. Out of this arose the sets inscribed simply in Latin 'Pro Patria' (for the fatherland) which have been issued each year since 1952. At first they continued the tradition of earlier charity sets by having a quasi-com-memorative nature, but more recent issues have been frankly thematic, like the Pro Juventute stamps.

The Swiss set the pattern for other countries making regular charity issues. This is the pattern favoured by the Benelux countries which issue children's stamps around the Christmas season and a more general charity issue about mid-summer. The German Federal Republic and West Berlin issue stamps inscribed *Wohlfahrts-marke* (welfare stamp), *Weihnachtsmarke* (Christmas stamp) or *Jugendmarke* (youth stamp), with postal values and charity premiums and, like their counterparts in other parts of Europe, have run through the entire gamut of the themes that have found most favour with stamp collectors. These stamps are the direct descendants of annual charity issued inscribed *Nothilfe* (emergency aid) which first appeared in

1924. French charity stamps began with issues in 1914 bearing a surcharge in aid of the Red Cross – a widespread practice during the First World War. They were followed by a long series of 1917 in aid of war orphans. This set was re-issued with new values and colours in 1922 and 1926 and was then succeeded by annual issues in aid of the sinking fund to reduce the national debt (*caisse d'amortissement*). In the 1930s sets were issued regularly in aid of unemployed intellectuals, with occasional issues designed to raise funds for war victims, the new postal museum and the birthrate development campaign. These were gradually consolidated from 1940 onwards into a national relief fund series. This continued for several years after the Second World War, but from 1950 on-wards there was a separate issue on behalf of the Red Cross. In 1958 the national relief fund series was transformed into a fund raiser for the Red Cross, continuing to appear in midsummer with the same cultural and historical themes as before. The existing Red Cross pair, however, also con-tinued to appear around the Christmas season. The only difference between the two annual issues is that the summer set makes no reference to the Red Cross, whereas the winter pair in-corporates the Red Cross emblem.

The Red Cross (and its Muslim counterpart, the Red Crescent) has been the beneficiary of countless charity stamps from every part of the world and a high proportion of the issues made at the present day refer specifically to this organization. Like France, Finland has been one of the most faithful producers of Red Cross charity stamps, with annual issues since 1930. In 1946 a second annual issue commenced, with premiums in aid of tuberculosis funds. A dual system continued till the late 1960s but since then one charity set has been issued, alternating between tuberculosis and the Red Cross.

The scourge of tuberculosis has inspired charity stamps from a number of countries, the most notable issues having come from the Philippines. In 1929 New Zealand issued a stamp portraying a nurse and bearing the slogan, 'Help stamp out tuberculosis'. This stamp had a postal value of 1d and a charity premium of the same value. It was re-issued the following year with an identical design, apart from the caption, which now took the more positive line 'Help promote health'. The Cross of Lorraine, international anti-tuberculosis symbol, appeared on this stamp, as it had in 1929, and was retained for a pair of stamps issued in 1931 showing a smiling boy, but now the caption proclaimed simply 'Health' – in larger lettering than the country name. The 'Smiling Boys' of 1931 were more than people could afford, since New Zealand was in the grip of a depression, and relatively few of them were sold. Today they are worth about £100 each, either mint or used! New Zealand persevered with the health stamps, though reverting to a single stamp in 1932, and it was not until 1938 that a pair was again issued. Sets of three appeared in 1955 and 1956 but this did not become a regular occurrence till 1974. The neo-classical imagery of the earlier issues gave way to more realistic depiction of children at work and play and this has continued to the present day. Royal children have been a popular subject since Princesses Elizabeth and Margaret Rose appeared on the triangular stamps of 1943. The stamps of 1945 and 1947 featured the statues of Peter Pan in Kensington Gardens and Eros in Piccadilly, London.

There is some tendency to be sceptical about the extent to which charity stamps are used on the ordinary mail of a country and there is a sneaking feeling that the bulk of the issue is purchased by the international philatelic fraternity. This is certainly not the case with the New Zealand health stamps which are extensively used on private and business correspondence. The money raised from their sale goes to provide health camps and recreational facilities for young people. It is surprising that health stamps have not spread to other countries, although Fiji issued them on a couple of occasions (1951 and 1954).

A grim reflection of the age in which we live is the growing number of stamps issued in aid of refugees. The United Nations designated 1960 as World Refugee Year and many of the stamps issued at that time bore premiums in aid of

refugee funds. At that time the refugee problem was largely confined to Hungarians displaced by the 1956 uprising, Palestinians in the Gaza Strip and South Moluccans who fled to Holland when Indonesia became independent. Since then the Palestinian problem has grown and other upheavals have provided their quota of refugees: Cypriot Greeks, Bangladeshis, Vietnamese, Cambodians, Laotians, Kurds, and now the Pathans from war-torn Afghanistan. Several

One of the world's most popular charity series, the health stamps issued annually by New Zealand since 1929 (112%)

countries issued charity stamps on behalf of the Hungarian refugees in 1956–7, but East Germany retaliated with stamps raising funds for the Egyptian victims of Anglo-French aggression at Suez and a stamp in aid of 'socialist' Hungary. Subsequent stamps from the Communist bloc raised money for the Vietnamese, and many Arab countries have assisted the Palestinians by means of charity stamps. Often these stamps are used as a political medium and their charitable purpose is sometimes obscured.

Compulsory charity stamps

So far all the stamps discussed in this chapter have been purely voluntary. In some cases, however, charity has been obligatory. Bulgaria wished to establish a sanatorium for postal and telegraph employees and hit upon a novel method of raising funds. Between 1925 and 1942 delivery of letters on Sundays could only be effected if the mail was franked with special Sunday delivery stamps in addition to the normal postage. The money from the sale of the Sunday stamps went to the sanatorium fund. The stamps depicted the proposed sanatorium and recreational facilities for postmen and their families.

During the First World War many countries raised money for the war effort by increasing postal rates. Because this was regarded as a temporary measure it was often accomplished by means of special stamps, inscribed or overprinted 'War tax' or 'War stamp', whose use was compulsory alongside the ordinary issues. This practice was widespread in the British Empire – though not in Britain itself. The idea was probably borrowed from Spain which had various war-tax stamps from the Carlist rebellions of the 1870s, through the Spanish-American War of 1898 to the Civil War of the 1930s. Neighbouring Portugal had a similar system of stamps whose use was compulsory on certain days of the year as an additional postal tax on internal mail. Ordinary definitives overprinted *Assistência* were issued in 1911. Later issues raised money for the Lisbon Fête in 1913, for the poor in general and war veterans in particular. The last of these charity tax stamps appeared in 1928 to raise funds for the national Olympic team. Failure to use these stamps on the compulsory days resulted in letters being surcharged with special postage due stamps.

Compulsory charity stamps have been widely used by many Latin American countries. Colombia issued obligatory tax stamps on behalf of the Red Cross from 1935 to 1970, but at other times of the year Colombians were required to use curious little stamps which raised money for the Post Office rebuilding fund. These tiny stamps, with their view of the proposed new Post Office in Bogotá, first appeared in 1939 and continued at annual intervals till 1952. Due to a shortage of ordinary postage stamps some of the last issue were used for normal postal purposes. Haiti has used compulsory charity stamps to raise funds for the literacy campaign, while Costa Rica has made such stamps obligatory on Christmas mail. Yugoslavia has issued stamps since the Second World War for compulsory use at certain periods in aid of the Red Cross and similar charity stamps have also been used for Children's Week, Solidarity Week and the ubiquitous Olympic Appeal. Failure to use these stamps has resulted, as in Portugal, in the application of special postage-due stamps, sometimes resembling the obligatory stamps but in different colours and inscribed 'Porto' (postage due). Another assiduous user of these enforced charity stamps was Romania which, at various times, issued them for soldiers' families, social welfare, aviation, child welfare and cultural funds, often with appropriately inscribed postage due stamps.

Turkey and Iran have both used labels, semi-official stamps and postal tax stamps to raise funds for the Red Crescent and medical services in general. Use of these stamps was compulsory on mail at certain periods. India raised money for Bengali refugees by overprinting a definitive stamp (itself publicizing the family-planning campaign) with 'Refugee Relief' and making its use compulsory on all mail. Recipients of mail from Bahrain in recent years were mystified by a blue label whose use appears to be compulsory. It denotes a 5 fils levy in aid of the Palestinian war

right **Charity stamps intended for compulsory use on mail during certain periods: Cyprus (refugee relief), West Germany (Berlin airlift fund), India (refugee relief), Costa Rica (children's village fund), Iran (Red Crescent), Greece (Patmos monastery restoration), and Bahrain (Palestine relief fund).** (88%)

effort. When the Russians blockaded West Berlin in 1948 the cost of mounting the airlift of supplies was defrayed by a compulsory 2-pfennig tax on all correspondence in West Germany and this was denoted by a tiny blue stamp inscribed *Berlin Notopfer Steuermarke* (emergency victims tax stamp). Long after the blockade ended this tax stamp was still obligatory and doubtless raised a considerable sum to assist the economic recovery of Germany in the early 1950s.

6 Booklets, coils, miniature sheets and composite stamps

The first stamps of the world were issued in sheets of 240. The inscriptions in the margins of sheets of the Penny Black indicated that the price per label was 1d, the price per row of twelve was 1s and the price per sheet was £1. Thus the sheet layout was dictated by the £sd system of currency then in existence. Countries with a decimal system of currency favoured sheets of 100 or 200 stamps which facilitated stock-taking and accountancy. Broadly speaking this system has been retained for definitives down to this day, but as many countries now use much larger sizes for their definitive stamps, paradoxically the sheet sizes have tended to become smaller. The large pictorial definitives, as well as many commemoratives, are issued in sheets of 50, 20 or even as few as 10 stamps. Although this was originally designed for the convenience of counter clerks, postal administrations soon discovered that this encouraged philatelists to collect entire sheets of stamps. This is often encouraged by lavishing more attention on the sheet margins. In addition to the various technical markings (discussed in Anatomy of a Stamp, p. 42) found on the selvedge there has been a tendency towards greater ornamentation of the margin so that the sheet, as a whole, becomes more desirable than its component stamps.

Sheets of stamps may be divided for the convenience of the counter clerks into panes (usually quarter sheets). Many of the early British stamps printed by De La Rue were given a much wider vertical margin on one side (the so-called wing margin) so that the clerk could see at a glance where the sheet should be folded. Unfortunately many collectors of Victorian times disliked wing-margined stamps for their lack of symmetry and cut off the offending margin. Today's philatelists realize that the wing-margined stamps are scarcer than ordinary specimens and they now tend to rate a premium. Some colonial stamps were printed in sheets whose panes were separated by a 'gutter' of blank paper. Stamps from rows adjoining this gutter, with the piece of blank paper between them, were known as 'interpanneau pairs'. Because the gutters were primarily for the convenience of the postal staff, who were often ordered to tear them off before selling the stamps, they are often quite rare. The use of gutters was revived in Britain in 1972 and

has been a feature of commemoratives since then. This has given rise to a mania for collecting gutter pairs, particular emphasis being laid on the 'traffic light' gutter pair. 'Traffic lights' is the nickname for the colour blobs used as a check in multicolour printing. These blobs have now been removed from the gutter, though they still appear in the sheet corner, and it is likely that the very high value placed on the 'traffic light' gutter pairs will drop as interest in this phenomenon declines.

Booklets

The sale of stamps to the public in a form designed to provide greater convenience has given rise to several distinct variations. Luxemburg was the first country to issue stamps in handy-sized booklets; though De La Rue had experimented with this method of vending revenue

below left **Coil strip of German stamps showing different denominations side by side and a label encouraging postal savings (64%)**

below right **The covers of stamp booklets range from the purely functional to the pictorial and colourful**

stamps in the 1870s the idea was rejected at the time. Germany, Belgium, France, the United States and Canada were among the early users of booklets, while Britain adopted the idea in 1904. The first British books contained 2s worth of stamps but were sold for 2s 0½d, the additional halfpenny defraying the cost of the thin card covers. As this was inconvenient to the public the price dropped to 2s and the cost of the booklet itself was covered by replacing one of the half-penny stamps by a bit of paper bearing a St Andrew's cross. Soon, however, postal admini-strations realized that they could sell the space on the covers and the pages of interleaving to com-mercial advertisers and this proved to be a lucrative business that more than covered the cost of booklet production. Even the occasional space in the booklet panes themselves was used for advertisements.

Booklets were produced from special printings of the stamps, often arranged so that different denominations were side by side (or *se-tenant*, to give the French term now commonly used by collectors). British stamps for booklets were printed in large sheets in which alternate panes were inverted. This was to make it easier for the printers to see where the panes should be divided, but occasional mistakes were perpetrated and this resulted in a few lucky customers getting booklets with misplaced panes, so that some stamps were upside down in relation to their neighbours (again a French term, *tête-bêche*, is used to describe this phenomenon). Since British stamps were printed on watermarked paper up to 1968 it follows that half the booklet stamps had an upright watermark and half had an in-verted watermark – a variation that philatelists constantly looked for. Faulty trimming by the guillotine which separated the booklets often results in clipped perforations and such stamps tend to be worth less than perfect specimens.

Though intended mainly for definitive stamps, booklets have sometimes contained commemo-ratives: the British Silver Jubilee series of 1935 was a noteworthy example. Australia has pro-duced a number of commemorative sets in small format which were only issued in booklets. This medium was used for the Famous Australians series launched in 1968. Conversely Australia released uncut sheets of a Royal Visit stamp of 1963, and this produced some curious varieties with either a wide margin on one side, or pairs with no perforations between them.

Coils

Booklets may be sold over the post office counter but nowadays they are often dispensed from coin-operated slot machines. The same principle is used to sell loose stamps which are emitted in a continuous coil. Coils of stamps have also been widely used in office dispensers. The earliest coils were produced from strips of stamps taken from sheets, a portion of the sheet margin being used to join one strip to the next. Coil-join pairs are

much sought after by philatelists. A later de-velopment was to print stamps in continuous coils of several hundred stamps. British stamps of this type had perforations on all four sides, but their true identity was revealed by their sideways watermark, and early examples are now highly desirable. In most countries, however, perfora-tions were only used between each stamp, and the outer sides were left imperforate. American and Canadian coils, for example, may be found perforated horizontally and imperforate verti-cally, or vice versa. Germany seems to have led the way with coils containing stamps of different values side by side, and even occasional labels bearing political slogans. *Se-tenant* strips made up of stamps of different denominations are now quite widespread in many countries, the total value being that of the coin required to activate the vending machine. Coils are best suited to small-format definitives, and some countries, such as Australia, New Zealand, Gibraltar and Barbados, which normally use large pictorial definitives, have had to introduce small-format stamps for slot machines. Commemoratives and other special issues are not normally dispensed in this manner, a notable exception being Sweden, all of whose stamps since the 1930s have only been available in coil or booklet form.

Miniature sheets

For the sake of convenience many of the world's charity stamps (e.g. New Zealand 'healths' and French Red Cross stamps) are sold in booklets or miniature sheets. The latter originated in Luxemburg in 1923 when a 10-franc stamp was issued in small sheets each containing a single stamp. In the early years definitive stamps (often in strips or blocks of four) were released in this form as souvenirs of philatelic exhibitions, but more recently many commemorative sets have been released in miniature sheets containing one of each value. Though long resisted as an un-necessary gimmick, there is hardly a country that has not issued a miniature sheet, and even Britain has produced some since 1978. Such sheets are often sold at a premium, the additional sum being used for exhibition funds and chari-ties. Considerable ingenuity has been shown in many cases in filling the marginal paper with illustrations that augment the design of the stamp or stamps.

British booklet pane showing different denominations side by side (66%)

right **1963 East German composite stamp marking the second 'team' manned space flight** (127%)

7 Postal stationery

Mention has already been made of the Mulready wrappers and envelopes which Britain introduced along with the Penny Black and Twopence Blue in 1840, and how several countries originally preferred prestamped stationery to adhesives. Although adhesive stamps have always been more flexible and convenient to the public, most postal administrations have produced stationery. Victorian philatelists collected stamped envelopes, postcards and wrappers avidly and there were even special catalogues devoted to the subject. But at the beginning of this century general collectors, overwhelmed by the sheer bulk of stationery, abandoned it and concentrated on adhesives. In recent years, however, as collectors have been forced to abandon a general approach to the hobby and specialize in one or two countries, stationery has come back into favour. The specialist takes an interest in every aspect of his chosen country's philately – and that includes the full range of postal stationery, as well as booklets, coils, miniature sheets and even complete sheets.

Postal stationery is best collected intact, though there is a certain vogue in the United States for 'cut-outs' of the imprinted stamp alone. Cut-outs are virtually useless to the specialist since much of the interest and value of stationery lies in the variations in the inscriptions and other markings found on the address side of postcards or the reverse of envelopes.

The earliest stationery consisted of letter sheets (which could be folded and sealed in the traditional manner), envelopes and wrappers. The Mulready pictorial design was not emulated in other countries and from 1841 onwards even Britain stuck to plain stationery with utilitarian inscriptions and imprinted or embossed stamps. The latter are often modified versions of designs used for adhesive stamps and add another dimension to the study of the adhesives. Special envelopes for registered letters spread gradually from the 1860s onwards. In this instance the embossed stamp was often struck on the back flap of the envelope, and adhesive stamps prepaying the postage were affixed to the front. This style survived in some colonial territories well into the present century.

Postcards

Postcards were invented by Emmanuel Herrmann of Austria in 1869 and spread rapidly to other countries the following year. At first only official stationery cards with imprinted or embossed stamps were permitted, but gradual relaxation of the regulations led to the development of private postcards and ultimately, in the 1890s, to picture postcards. Stamped postcards have been extensively used by many countries to promote tourism, since they provide a con-

venient medium for summer visitors. Such cards may be found with a picture on the address side, near the stamp, as well as or instead of the usual picture on the front. Austria, Germany, Czechoslovakia, France and Switzerland are notable exponents of the tourist stamped postcard, but in recent years Australia has gone a stage farther with cards whose stamps reproduce in miniature the picture found on the other side. The United States began publishing postcards with attractive vignettes during the Bicentennial celebrations and this practice is likely to be greatly extended in the future.

Stamped postcards were originally favoured as a commemorative medium and there are numerous examples from as far afield as New South Wales and Salvador, New Zealand and Sweden around the turn of the century. Though this practice declined as adhesive commemoratives became more fashionable it has not entirely disappeared. The United States, in particular, produces a wide range of cards and envelopes with stamps of a commemorative nature, while the Soviet Union produces stationery with imprinted definitives, but with the vignettes commemorating all manner of events and personalities.

Air letters

One form of stationery that has enjoyed an immense following since its inception is the air letter or aerogramme. This convenient, lightweight airmail stationery was invented by Douglas Gumley and first used in Iraq in 1933. The idea was taken up by Britain during the Second World War, initially as a Forces Air Letter and subsequently extended to civilian use. There were also special (and now much sought after) versions for prisoners of war. After the war air letters were adopted by other countries and are now almost universally used. In some countries, such as New Zealand, they are produced by the post office without impressed stamps and therefore require adhesives to be affixed, but almost everywhere else they are part of the range of official postal stationery and are issued with specially printed stamps. Australia

The world's first postcard, adopted by Austria in 1869

led the way in issuing special air letters for Christmas, though Britain had commemorative air letters for the 1948 Olympic Games and the Coronation in 1953. A more recent development has been the tourist aerogramme – now widely used in Scotland, to a lesser extent in Wales and not at all in England, though two were issued experimentally in the 1960s. Pictorial aerogrammes have been issued in recent years in many countries, from Sweden to Sri Lanka (Ceylon), from Canada to Zimbabwe (Rhodesia).

Wrappers and uprated items

There are many other kinds of postal stationery: newspaper bands or wrappers date from the 1850s, though they were not adopted in Britain till 1870. Letter cards developed at the turn of the century and included some unusual types from Newfoundland with an inner letter sheet. Reply-paid postcards were widely used in the 1880s and 1890s and, in fact, survived till the 1960s, though there seems to have been little use for them and used examples are quite elusive, though unused cards, with both outward and inward cards intact, are not uncommon. Some European countries have had special stamped envelopes for telegrams; France even had distinctive stationery in connection with a pneumatic-tube post. Of particular interest is postal stationery that has been uprated as a result of increases in postal rates. This may be done by surcharging the imprinted stamps, by printing a new stamp or some other device alongside, or by adding adhesive stamps to make up the required amount. As such uprated items are generally short-lived they are worth looking out for.

Presentation packs and PHQ cards

Two collectable items now available from the British Post Office which may be considered under the heading of stationery are presentation packs and PHQ cards. Presentation packs, as the name suggests, are special display units containing sets of stamps, together with attractive packaging and filler cards containing background information to the stamps. These packs have been produced for every commemorative issue since the Shakespeare series of 1964, and although they were originally intended merely as a convenient method of packaging stamps for sale to the public they have become eminently collectable in their own right: some of the earlier packs are worth considerably more than the stamps themselves. Presentation packs have been issued by some other countries, Australia being a leading exponent of this. Many countries also produce an annual pack, containing all the definitive and commemorative stamps of the past year, with an explanatory booklet. These are now widely used as Christmas gifts.

PHQ cards take their name from the abbreviation for British Postal Headquarters in London whose imprint appears on the reverse with their serial number. They are postcards with enlarged reproductions of commemorative stamps. Ideally the collector should try to get them used on the first day of the new stamp, with the appropriate commemorative cancelled by the first day postmark, but even the unused cards (especially the earlier issues) are highly prized. These cards have only been in existence since 1973, but such is the demand for them that already it would cost a great deal of money to purchase a complete set.

right **British Air Mail Letter Card, with Field Post Office cancellation, RAF censor stamp and civilian censorship label – the forerunner of the modern air letter or aerogramme**

far right **Pictorial air letters are now widely used as a tourist souvenir**

below right **Special pictorial air letter issued for Christmas greetings by Australia**

below far right **Special postcard issued by France in connection with a service by pneumatic tube**

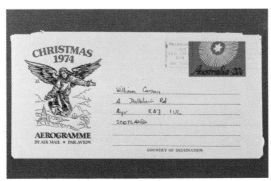

ß Airmails

Nowadays airmail is something we take very much for granted. The vast bulk of international mail is transported by air and a significant proportion of internal mail goes by aircraft at some point on its journey. In many cases only the really long-distance mail requires the use of special labels, postal markings or stationery, so it is not always apparent that an envelope or postcard has actually gone by air. Many countries continue to issue definitive stamps specially inscribed for use on airmail, but this practice has declined as more and more mail goes by air as a matter of course. Moreover, many of the modern stamps inscribed *Correo Aéreo, Par Avion, Luftpost* or their equivalent in other languages do not have designs that allude to aviation. Before the Second World War, however, when transmission by air was the exception rather than the rule, greater attention was paid to designing air stamps that looked the part, with symbolism of flight, pictures of soaring birds, vignettes of identifiable aircraft or occasionally portraits of the heroes and heroines of pioneer aviation. The inauguration of a new service was heralded by commemorative stamps and there were special postmarks and cachets (rubber stamps) used at airports and for inaugural flights. Much of the glamour and romance has gone out of aviation, but new routes are continually being opened up, new and faster jets brought into service, and still there is some scope for the intrepid lone aviator, so that aerophilately continues to provide an abundance of new material for the collector. The designs of aerogrammes are constantly changing, and a significant proportion of modern airmail stamps commemorate the anniversaries of historic flights, so it is hardly surprising that this is one of the most popular facets of stamp collecting.

The Wright Brothers made their first flight in December 1903 and the development of commercial aviation is essentially a product of the twentieth century. Yet surprisingly enough, airmail existed at a much earlier date. There are isolated examples of letters having been carried by balloon from the late eighteenth century onwards, but this system was first used on a highly organized basis during the sieges of Paris and Metz during the Franco-Prussian War of 1870–1. There were even special letter sheets inscribed *Par ballon monté* (by manned balloon) which are the forerunners of the modern aerogramme. Although a few of these mail-carrying balloons drifted into the enemy lines or were lost in the sea the great majority landed safely in friendly territory and their precious cargo was delivered to the addressees. Mail was flown into beleaguered Paris by pigeons which had tiny pellicules of microfilm attached to their tail coverts. The microfilms were mounted on slides and projected on to a screen in a room filled with clerks whose

task it was to transcribe them. The transcriptions were placed in envelopes and forwarded to the addressee in the usual way.

The airmails of the Siege of Paris rank as the world's first practical system but once the exigencies of war were removed there was no incentive to continue or develop the idea. Pigeon posts were, in fact, used at the turn of the century to communicate between Auckland, New Zealand, and its offshore islands. The Great Barrier Pigeon Service and the Marotiri Copper Syndicate both issued special stamps and stationery, including flown flimsies, until the extension of the telegraph services rendered this method of communication obsolete.

Balloons were of little use, except in the direst

above **French marines guarding a group of manned balloons prior to lift-off, during the siege of Paris, 1870**

left **'Le Petit Journal', one of several miniature, lightweight newspapers produced for airmail transmission during the siege of Paris**

emergency, since they could not be steered. In the early years of this century, however, August von Parseval and Ferdinand von Zeppelin experimented with dirigible balloons and the various trial and exhibition flights before the First World War are recalled by the souvenir cards, semi-official stamps, labels, postmarks and cachets associated with such airships as the *Schwaben* and the *Viktoria Luise*. At the same time enormous developments took place in the heavier-than-air machines and flying became the rage in America and Europe. Many countries staged aviation meetings and flying demonstrations and though very few of the souvenir postcards and envelopes associated with them were actually flown they are of immense interest to aerophilatelists. Aerial parcel services operated in Ohio (1910) and Northampton (1911), and in the same period there were experimental mail flights in Italy (1910), India, England and the United States (1911). These were more in the nature of stunts and it was not until the First World War that serious attempts were made to fly mail on a regular basis. In 1915 letters and cards were flown out of Przemyśl by the Austrians, when the fortress was besieged by the Russians, and other military airmail services were subsequently established.

The first official airmail issues

In 1917 Italy instituted a regular airmail service between Rome and Turin. Express delivery stamps were overprinted for this purpose and are regarded as the world's first official airmail issue. Many of the air stamps up to the late 1920s were semi-official of limited validity, or were entirely unofficial, being produced by the promoters of

private air services. In 1918 the United States issued a set of three stamps for airmail and featured a Curtiss Jenny biplane. One sheet of the 24-cent stamps, printed in red and blue, was discovered with the centre upside down. Today examples of the 'Inverted Jenny' rank among the greatest rarities of aerophilately. Germany issued two air stamps in 1919, following Austria which had an overprinted series in 1918. Thereafter air stamps for regular usage were issued by Switzerland, Colombia and Japan (1919); Danzig, Spain and Syria (1920); the Netherlands, Latvia and China (1921); Mexico and Russia (1922); the Lebanon (1924); Denmark, Honduras, Poland and South Africa (1925); Costa Rica, Egypt and the Philippines (1926); Chile, Cuba, France, Peru, Brazil and Bulgaria (1927); Canada, Ecuador, Panama, Argentina and Romania (1928); and Guatemala, Haiti, India, Nicaragua and Paraguay (1929). In the 1930s airmail stamps spread to most other countries. Oddly enough, Britain has never issued adhesives specifically for this purpose, although some collectors regard the Elizabethan 1s 3d and 1s 6d stamps of the 1950s as filling this role, and the higher values of more recent commemorative sets are intended primarily for postage to the A, B, and C airmail zones.

Internal airmails

The greatest use of airmail stamps today is in those countries which, because of their size, rely on airmail as a quicker but more expensive way of conveying mail from one part to another. Canada, the United States, Mexico, Chile and Colombia all have a long history of special stamps for internal airmails, though Canada has dropped this pratice in recent years. Chile issued stamps inscribed Correo Aéreo Chile for use on external airmails and similar designs inscribed Correos de Chile/Linea Aérea Nacional (Posts of Chile/National Air Line) for internal airmails. Internal airmails in Colombia were in the hands of a company with the lengthy title of Sociedad Colombo-Alemana de Transportes Aéreos (Colombian-German Society for Air Transport), usually known from its initials as SCADTA. In the 1920s it was possible to hand in mail destined for Colombian addresses at Colombian embassies and consulates in many parts of the world. Envelopes were franked by the stamps of the country of origin, and special SCADTA stamps overprinted with the initial of the country. These stamps may be found with the initials EU (Estados Unidos = United States), A (Alemania = Germany), E (España = Spain), Su (Suecia = Sweden) as well as the more easily recognizable initials of other countries.

Stamps for famous flights

The most fascinating (and often the rarest) of all airmail stamps are those produced in connection with epic flights that spanned the world in the decade following the First World War. Several

Airmail stamps of the world. *Top row:* stylized aircraft or symbols of flight; *2nd–3rd rows:* identifiable aircraft, often incorporating scenery; *last stamp 3rd row* **and** *4th row:* mythology, religion and folklore are subjects that lend themselves to an aviation interpretation; *5th row:* historic aircraft, flora and fauna, and astronauts comprise some of the varied motifs of modern air stamps (61%)

attempts were made to bridge the Atlantic and on each occasion Newfoundland dispatched a quantity of mail with the aviators, obligingly overprinting various stamps for the purpose. The greatest rarities are those associated with the flights by Hawker and Mackenzie-Grieve, Martinsyde, Raynham and Morgan, and the Marchese de Pinedo, whereas the special stamp for the first *successful* flight, by Sir John Alcock and Sir Arthur Whitten Brown, is much cheaper. Newfoundland had overprinted airmail stamps for several later flights, including the trans-Atlantic flight of the giant Dornier DO X and the Balbo mass flight. The most ambitious series of stamps for a single flight was that issued by Italy in 1933 in connection with the latter flight – by an armada of 24 planes, headed by Italo Balbo. Twenty of these planes carried souvenir mail and the stamps in each case bore the abbreviated name of the appropriate pilot, the most desirable items being those with General Balbo's own stamps. Mail was flown from England to Australia by Ross and Keith Smith in 1919 but a semi-official stamp was not added to the covers until the mail reached its destination. Other epic flights of the 1920s were sometimes honoured by special stamps but more often special postmarks and cachets were used. Disappointingly no provision was made for mail to be carried officially by Charles Lindbergh on his solo flight of 1927, but the numerous goodwill flights of Colonel Lindbergh to Latin America were often commemorated by special stamps issued by the countries he visited. Several stamps were also issued in honour of Amelia Earhart, and Australia and New Zealand issued stamps for Kingsford Smith and Charles Ulm.

Airmail flown by the famous pioneer aviators is now exceedingly expensive, but most collectors can afford the first flight covers and other souvenirs produced by the commercial airlines that developed from 1919 onwards. As these covers and cards are often postmarked on arrival at their destination, and bear elaborate cachets with the names of the staging points and even maps of the route, they tend to be very colourful. Souvenir covers are also produced in connection with new types of aircraft and already quite a large collection could be made of stamps, covers, cards, postmarks and cachets associated with the Anglo-French Concorde.

The 1930s were dominated by the great trans-Atlantic and world flights of the giant German airships *Graf Zeppelin* and *Hindenburg*. These aerial monsters captured the imagination of the world and many countries, from Russia to Argentina, from Finland to the United States, issued stamps in their honour. Interest in airships waned after the spectacular destruction of the *Hindenburg* while landing at Lakehurst, N.J., in 1937, but although this leisurely method of aviation has since been overtaken by intercontinental jets there have been attempts to revive airships for air freight if not passengers.

Ballooning as a sport continues and there have been numerous occasions, from the Gordon Bennett Balloon Races of the 1920s, when souvenir airmail has been carried by this means.

V-mail, airgraphs and pigeon posts

During the Second World War the French idea of microfilming letters for transmission by air was revived, though aircraft rather than pigeons were used. The microfilms were developed at the destination and enlarged prints forwarded to the addressees in special envelopes. This system was known as V-mail in the United States and as airgraphs in Britain and both the special envelopes and the photographic letters themselves are much sought after nowadays. Mention has already been made of aerogrammes whose development was greatly stimulated during the war, though they have since received almost universal application. Another aspect of aerophilately that was developed in wartime concerns aerial propaganda leaflets, and the collection and study of these fascinating documents has given rise to a separate branch of aerophilately known as psychological warfare, or psywar for short. Leaflets of this type are believed to have been delivered by artillery shells in the Napoleonic wars, but most of the examples now collected date from the First World War when the Italian poet Gabriele d'Annunzio bombed Vienna with leaflets containing his own patriotic poetry. Leaflets were dropped by the ton on both belligerent and neutral countries during the Second World War, and since then use of this method of putting across a message has been noted in Vietnam, Northern Ireland and other trouble spots around the world.

Pigeon posts have also been revived from time to time, usually in connection with fairs and exhibitions. The best known of these pigeon mails comes from India where this was a popular stunt in the 1920s and 1930s, and the specially printed pigeongrams of that period are now in demand. Pigeon posts have also been organized in more recent years as charity fund raisers. Before the Second World War mail was sometimes flown by gliders in connection with sporting contests in Germany, Austria and Britain, and since the war similar events have taken place in the Netherlands, Liechtenstein, Yugoslavia and Poland. A more recent development is hang gliding and there have been instances of mail, bearing special postmarks and cachets, flown across the English Channel or even from the summit of Ben Nevis in Scotland by this means.

Mails by rotorcraft

Autogiros and later helicopters were developed in the 1930s as a convenient method of transporting passengers from airports to city centres and inevitably mail was carried on some of these flights. After the war the use of helicopters for short-haul mail flights was greatly extended. Special envelopes and cachets are known in

John Stewart
demonstrating some
of the mail-carrying
rockets used by the
Paisley Rocketeers;
a cover flown by
aquajet rocket from
Castle Stalker to
Portnacroish, 1972

Many current or
recent airmail stamps
have little indication,
other than inscription,
to denote their special
usage! Neil
Armstrong's 'first
step for mankind' on
a Mexican air stamp
(264 %)

airmail, the Coronation Aerial Post of 1911. Sweden, Switzerland, Italy, Belgium, the United States and New Zealand were among the earliest exponents of helicopter mail. Nowadays all mail to and from the North Sea oil rigs is flown by helicopter and there have been souvenir covers and cachets in connection with this service.

Mails by rocket

Rocket mail is probably the ultimate form of communication, yet this has been in existence for more than half a century. Experiments with mail-carrying projectiles were made in Austria as long ago as 1928 by Friedrich Schmiedl and over the ensuing decade a number of rocket flights were carried out, with special stationery, postal markings and even stamps. The idea soon spread to Germany where Reinhold Tiling and Gerhard Zucker made several successful launches. In 1934 Zucker visited England and carried out rocket mails at Rottingdean on the Sussex Downs. Later he went to the Outer Hebrides and attempted to fly mail by rocket from the island of Scarp to Harris, but the projectile exploded and many of the letters got rather scorched! Zucker subsequently carried out rocket flights with souvenir mail in Belgium, Holland, Switzerland and other European countries before settling down to research that culminated in the German V-1 and V-2 guided missiles of the Second World War. Oddly enough, India witnessed the greatest number of mail-rocket flights before the war; special rocket stamps, labels, cards and covers were produced for these flights. Since the war most of the research in this field has been conducted in America by the Society of Applied Rocketry (SOAR) and in Britain by the Paisley Rocketeers led by John Stewart who has carried out a number of successful flights, including the celebrated trans-Atlantic flights between the Scottish mainland and the island of Seil. Because of the ban on the use of explosives in Britain, the Paisley Rocketeers have concentrated on the development of aqua-jets, using high-pressure water jets to propel their rockets. Quite a sizeable collection can be formed of the souvenir covers, cards, flimsies, stamps and labels produced in connection with these Scottish flights.

In 1969 the crew of Apollo 11 took to the moon a steel die for printing a special stamp. After landing on the moon, Neil Armstrong made an impression of this die on a piece of paper and thus created the first moon stamp. The die was returned to earth and later used in the production of stamps celebrating the mission. The astronauts also had with them an envelope bearing a proof of this stamp and this was then cancelled with a postmark inscribed 'Moon Landing USA' with the date Jul 20 1969 in the centre. Although the 10 cent stamp commemorating the event was intended for ordinary postage it may be regarded in time to come as a forerunner of interplanetary mail and astrophilately.

connection with the East Anglian helicopter service inaugurated by British European Airways in East Anglia in 1948. BEA even produced a helicopter stamp in 1961 for mail flights between London and Windsor, to commemorate the golden jubilee of the first official British

9 Stamps for special purposes

So far we have examined the four main classes of postage stamp: definitives, commemoratives, semi-postals and airmails. These terms are sometimes combined and you may find airmails that form part of a definitive series or a commemorative set – Switzerland had air stamps with a charity premium (*Pro Aero*), and many semi-postal or charity issues are also commemorative in character. In addition to these main classes, however, there are many other kinds of stamps which have been produced for special purposes. Collectors nickname them the 'end of book' stamps, from the custom adopted by many stamp catalogues of placing them at the end of the general lists of a country's stamps. By and large these are the stamps whose use is restricted in some way.

Purists argue that one class at least should not even be regarded as postage stamps at all since they did not prepay postage or indicate free postage. These are the labels inscribed 'Postage due' or 'To pay' or their equivalents in other languages. They are affixed to unpaid or underpaid mail, to letters posted irregularly or infringing postal regulations, and are also used to facilitate the collection of customs duty on parcels from abroad. These labels bear expressions of value, just like postage stamps, since the postmen who stick them on letters have to account for the money which they are required to recover from the addressee. France pioneered these unpaid letter stamps in 1859 with labels inscribed *A Percevoir* (to pay) and the amount due. These stamps spread to the French colonies and it is interesting to note that Guadeloupe actually had postage-due stamps eight years before it issued postage stamps. Other early users of these stamps included some of the German states, such as Bavaria which introduced stamps inscribed *Posttaxe* in 1862. Belgium and the Netherlands both adopted them in 1870, recognized by the Dutch words *Te Betalen* and, in the case of Belgium, its French equivalent *A Payer* as well. Switzerland introduced postage-due stamps in 1878, bereft of inscriptions and having no more than the numerals to indicate the amount due. The United States began issuing postage-due stamps a year later and since then

Stamps for special purposes: Yugoslavia (military post); Bosnia (postage due); Bosnia (Austrian imperial field post); Portugal (shooting club free frank); United States (parcel post, parcel postage due, airmail special delivery); Liberia (registration); Canada (registration). (153%)

all of these stamps, regardless of face value, have been printed in red, though the denominations since 1959 have been inserted in black.

Britain was slow to adopt these stamps – the first of them appeared in 1914. From then until the introduction of decimal coinage in the 1970s the same designs were retained, making British postage-dues one of the longest-running issues in philately. The combination of long life, uniform designs, often the same colour for every denomination, and a penchant for numerals or utilitarian motifs, explains the general neglect that these stamps have suffered, though finely used specimens are often elusive and examples correctly used on unpaid or underpaid covers and cards may be quite scarce in some cases. Apart from their rather mundane appearance they can usually be recognized by the prominence

given to the numerals of value, and by one or other of the following inscriptions: *A Payer* or *A Percevoir* (French-speaking countries), *Bajar porto* (Indonesia), *Chiffre Taxe* (France), *Deficit* (Spanish countries), *Doplata* (Poland), *Doplatit* or *Doplatne* (Czechoslovakia), *Efterporto* (Denmark), *Franqueo deficiente* (Latin America), *Lösen* (Sweden), *Multa* (Portuguese-speaking countries), *Multada* (Spanish), *Porteado* (Portuguese), *Porto* (Denmark, Hungary, Yugoslavia and German-speaking countries), *Portomarke* (Germany), *Portzegel* (Netherlands), *Postas le n'ioc* (Irish Republic), *Recouvrement* (France, Monaco), *Segnatasse* (Italy), *Sobreporte* or *Sobretasse* (Spanish), *Taxe* (French), *Takca* (Bulgaria), *Taksë* (Albania), *Tasa por cobrar* (Spanish), *Taxa de plata* (Romania), *Taxa devida* (Portugal), *Te Betaal* (South Africa), *Te Betalen*

Postage due stamps of France (the world's first, 1859), Tangier, Australia, United States, Ireland, United Kingdom, Hungary, Czechoslovakia, Guernsey, Danzig, Dahomey and Yugoslavia *(150%)*

(Belgium and the Netherlands), and *Vom Empfänger Einzuziehen* (Danzig). In recent years, however, more attractive designs have been used by Monaco and several countries of the French Community and this trend has since spread to other countries.

Newspaper stamps

Newspaper stamps are another large group which had their origins in the widespread principle of levying a tax on newspapers as a means of controlling the press. In Britain this was denoted by a red stamp printed on the top right-hand corner of the front page. Although primarily a 'tax on knowledge' it permitted newspapers to be transmitted free through the post, so long as they were registered at the General Post Office. The tax was abolished in 1855, but such imprinted stamps continued till 1870 for papers sent by post and are thus a form of postage stamp. From 1870 onwards most British papers made use of the stamped newspaper wrappers then introduced, though *The Times* clung to the archaic system of an impressed die. France issued adhesive stamps which combined a postal and a tax function. They are known as journal tax stamps and were affixed to the paper before printing, so that the typography acted as an effective cancellation. A similar practice was used for the stamps of Austria, inscribed *Zeitungsmarke* (newspaper stamp).

Many of the newspaper stamps of the world pose a problem to the beginner since they did not bear any form of inscription. This is especially true of many of the newspaper stamps from Austria, but they can be identified as Austrian from the portrait of Mercury that adorns them. Anonymous stamps showing a girl in provincial costume were issued by Bosnia in 1913 (then part of the Austrian empire, but now part of Yugoslavia). Czechoslovak newspaper stamps at least bore the name of the country though their purpose was not apparent. Earlier issues showed a dove, but postwar stamps showed a postman clutching a newspaper. Stamps overprinted 'Noviny' were also used on newspapers: others overprinted rather cryptically OT (*Otdelni tiskopis*) were intended for use on printed matter. Other newspaper stamps can be identified by the inclusion in their inscription of the following keywords: *Dagbladen* (Flemish), *Jornaes* (Portuguese), *Journaux* (French) or *Avisporto* (Danish). Probably the most spectacular of all newspaper stamps were those issued by the United States from 1865 to 1875; they measured 51 × 95 mm (2 × 3¾ in) and were the largest stamps in the world until recently. They were superseded by an extraordinary series running from 2 cents to $60 depicting mainly allegorical female figures, though Longfellow's heroine Minnehaha appeared on the top value. By contrast the halfpenny stamps issued by Britain and the Australian states, though not specifically inscribed for newspaper postage, were much

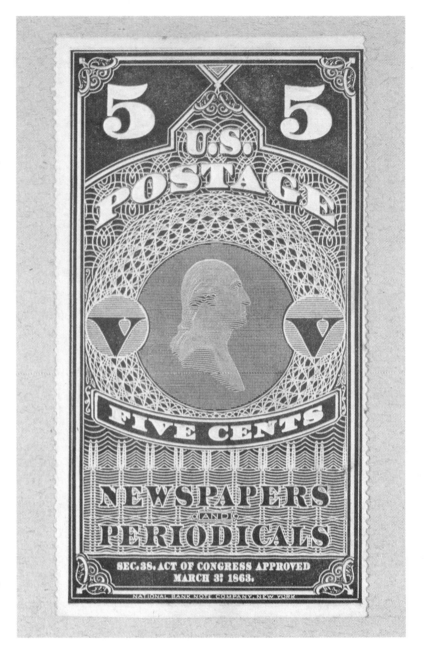

smaller than the average definitive. New Zealand alone issued a stamp expressly inscribed 'Newspaper Postage' (1873), the design being closely modelled on the British halfpenny stamp issued three years earlier.

Official mails

Penny Blacks were printed in 1840 with the letters VR (the royal monogram) in the upper corners instead of stars and were intended for use by government departments. They were never issued – though a few examples are known to have been used instead of ordinary postage stamps – and it was not until 1882 that Britain released some of the current definitives with the overprint 'I.R. Official' for use by the Inland Revenue department. Subsequently stamps were issued for other departments (Admiralty, Army, Board of Education, Office of Works and the Royal Household) and there was even an issue

United States newspaper stamp – until recently the world's largest stamp (150%)

Newspaper stamps from France, Austria, New Zealand, Sardinia, Bohemia and Portugal (171%)

Official mail stamps from India, Bulgaria, Philippines, Tanganyika, Australia, Peru, United States and Norway (actual size)

overprinted 'Govt. Parcels' for use on government parcels. These stamps were very strictly controlled and following a leakage to collectors they were abruptly withdrawn from use in 1904. They were later replaced by printed labels and stationery inscribed Official Paid, a system that is still in use.

Some of the Australian states made special provision for government mail. South Australia's 54 government departments used definitive stamps overprinted with their initials in various colours between 1868 and 1874, but subsequently stamps overprinted OS (official service) were introduced and this practice was adopted by the other states, and used by Australia in the years 1931–3. Since then the Australian states have used Australian definitives perforated with their initials. Argentina was a prolific issuer of overprinted stamps for use in different government offices, but the most ambitious series of all came from the United States. Known to collectors as the Departmentals, they were adopted in 1873 to check the abuse of the franking privilege. A separate series was produced in May of each year for each of the nine executive departments and, except for the Post Office series, these stamps portrayed famous Americans. Departmental stamps were discontinued in 1879 and since official envelopes have been used instead, though a series of stamps from 1 cent to $1 was issued in 1910–11 for use by the postal savings department.

Like Australia, Papua has had stamps overprinted OS, and in the Philippines stamps overprinted OB are used to denote official business. The initials OHMS were formerly perforated on Canadian stamps to signify 'On His Majesty's Service', and appeared as an overprint in 1949–50 but thereafter stamps were overprinted G (Government) until 1963 when official stamps were discontinued. Indian stamps were overprinted ON HMS between 1874 and 1909 but 'Service' appeared as an overprint on some stamps from 1866 to 1939 and this now appears in the inscription of special stamps for official use. Some of the Indian states used the overprint ON GS (Government Service), though Soruth used the Hindi form *Sarkari*. European countries have issued definitives with an overprint, or even

specially designed stamps, for official use from time to time. This usage can be identified by inscriptions such as *Dienstmarke* (Germany); *Tjeneste frimærke* (Denmark); *Tjänste frimärke* (Sweden); *Tjeneste frimerke* or *Offentlig sak* (Norway); as well as the word 'Official' and its variants. Württemberg issued stamps inscribed *Amtlicher Verkehr* (official traffic), *Bezirksmarke* (municipal stamp) or *Staatsmarke* (state stamp). Dutch stamps overprinted *Armenwet* denote use by the Poor Law Department. German stamps inscribed *Frei Durch Ablösung* were issued to government offices in Prussia and Baden in 1903–5 in order to assess the amount of revenue owed to the imperial postal service for government mail. A similar ploy was used by Thailand in 1963–4; stamps inscribed 'For government service statistical research' were compulsory on official correspondence to determine how much mail was handled by each department.

Parcel stamps

Parcel stamps have been issued by comparatively few countries, although those that do so have been quite prolific. Belgium issued a few stamps in 1928–33 for general parcels, but the vast bulk of the parcel stamps from 1879 to the present day (running to well over 400 different varieties) have been issued for use on parcels transmitted by the state railways. The post office parcel stamps were inscribed *Postcollo* (Flemish) and *Colis postal* (French), whereas the railway parcel stamps are inscribed *Spoorwegen/Chemins de Fer* ('railways' in Flemish and French). Those stamps with a posthorn motif in their design were sold over the post office counter in connection with a 'small parcels' service. The earlier stamps were rather monotonous in design, but since 1916 they have

become increasingly pictorial, usually featuring locomotives, railway stations and aspects of parcel handling. Bulgaria produced three sets of stamps during the Second World War that were inscribed, in Cyrillic, *Koletni pratki*: 'parcel post'. One set had an armorial motif, but the others showed the parcel service at work.

The United States established a government parcel post in 1913 and issued a series of pictorial stamps from 1 cent to $1. There was also a series of parcel postage-due stamps, but these were in use for only a few months. The parcel stamps themselves were withdrawn after a short period and ordinary definitives have been used ever since. Mexico has had parcel stamps (inscribed *Buitos postales*) since 1941, but among the countries of Latin America the most prolific has been Uruguay whose stamps even included special issues for agricultural produce (*Encomiendas de granja*). The most unusual parcel stamps are those issued by Italy, San Marino and the erstwhile Italian colonies. Inscribed *Pacchi postali*, they are issued in two parts. The left-hand portion, inscribed *Sul bollettino*, is affixed to a postal docket and the right-hand part, inscribed *Sulla ricevuta*, is affixed to the receipt handed to the sender.

Fiscal stamps

Adhesive stamps intended for fiscal purposes are known as revenues or fiscals. As a rule they are ignored by philatelists, but whenever they are authorized for postal use they come within the orbit of stamp collecting and are then known as postal fiscals. Such stamps were authorized in Britain in 1881; other examples include Ceylon's Postal Commission stamps of 1872–80, New Zealand's stamp duty and land deeds stamps from 1882 to 1914, and the 'arms' high values issued from 1931 to the present day. Many of the Australian states issued stamps inscribed 'Stamp Duty' for postage or revenue.

Special delivery stamps

Several countries have issued stamps for express and special delivery services, to denote the extra charges incurred by special handling. These stamps bear such inscriptions as *Exprès* (Canada, 1927–47); *Espresso* (Italy since 1903); *Urgente* (Spain since 1905); and *Entrega inmediata* (Latin American countries). Peruvian definitives were overprinted *Expreso* for this purpose. Apart from Canada, the only Commonwealth country to have issued Express Delivery stamps was New Zealand, from 1903 to 1939. The United States began issuing Special Delivery stamps in 1885. The first issue showed a running messenger and was inscribed 'Secures immediate delivery at a Special Delivery Office', but this was superseded by similar stamps three years later with the inscription emended to read 'at any post office'. By 1902 the messenger depicted on the stamps was mounted on a bicycle, and this was upgraded to a

Express or special delivery stamps: Italy, New Zealand, Canada, United States (114%)

motorcycle in 1922 and a motor van three years later. A design showing hands exchanging a letter was introduced in 1954 and since 1969 a symbolic design of arrows has been used. In 1925 the United States issued a set of five stamps inscribed 'Special Handling', the purpose being to give first-class priority to fourth-class mail. In 1934 stamps were issued for Special Delivery Airmail and depicted the great seal of the United States. (These stamps were actually designed by none other than the President, Franklin D. Roosevelt, himself a lifelong philatelist.) Some Colombian airmail stamps have borne an overprint *Extra rapido* to prepay the additional cost of sending inland mail by air.

Stamps for registered mail

Special stamps for use on registered letters were issued by Canada from 1875 to the end of the century and for a brief time the United States (1911–13). Several Latin American countries have had stamps that contained a space for the insertion of the registration serial number. This practice was adopted by Liberia in 1893, but from 1903 attractive pictorial designs were used. These stamps were issued in sets of five, each stamp bearing the name of one of the five principal towns in the country. These stamps were withdrawn in the 1940s. Registration labels, discussed in the section on Cinderella Philately (p. 58), have even been used as postage stamps in times of emergency. Various labels used in German New Guinea were seized by the invading Imperial forces in 1914 and surcharged 3d, with the royal monogram GRI and used as threepenny stamps. Some Latin American countries have also issued stamps to denote acknowledgment of receipt and can be recognized by the initials AR, for the Spanish *Aviso de recepción*. Colombia had a pair of stamps inscribed A (*Anotado*) and R (*Registro*) respectively, one covering the registration fee and the other the notification of receipt.

Other special-purpose stamps

There are many other miscellaneous stamps that may occasionally be encountered. Since 1891 New Zealand's Government Life Insurance Department has issued distinctive stamps featuring lighthouses. The Netherlands had special marine-insurance stamps which guaranteed the carriage of letters on board ship in fireproof, unsinkable safes (*drijvende brandkasten*). Argentina has had 'phonopostal' stamps prepaying the charges for the delivery of vocally recorded messages; these stamps had a gramophone record as their motif. The Dominican Republic issued a stamp in 1935 which had to be affixed to letters addressed to the President. Czechoslovakia in 1937 had Personal Delivery stamps. Italy has issued a number of stamps in connection with the pneumatic-tube post. Stamps inscribed *Retardo* have been issued by some Latin American countries to prepay late fees.

10 Beginning a stamp collection

The tremendous popularity of stamp collecting stems from the ease with which a collection can be started. In many countries today a rummage through the correspondence of the average family will yield a surprising number of different stamps. As this book is being written increased postal charges in Britain have brought the 10p and 12p stamps to the fore, but there are still plenty of 7p, 8p and 9p stamps being used up, with an assortment of low-value stamps to make up the amounts. Those who get mail from Scotland, Wales and Northern Ireland will also be familiar with the regional versions, with national emblems in the corner; those fortunate enough to have correspondents in Guernsey, Jersey, the Isle of Man and the Irish Republic will find an astonishing array of attractive, multicoloured definitives on their mail. Hard on the heels of the Christmas stamps has come the set of four featuring Wild Birds, and this has been shortly followed by the strip of five stamps depicting the Liverpool–Manchester railway of 1830. With commemorative sets appearing every other month there is plenty of interest and variety in modern British stamps. Most British people have at least one contact overseas and are thus familiar with the current definitives of the United States (cultural heritage), Canada (flowers), Australia (marine life and gemstones) or New Zealand (garden roses and Maori artifacts) – not to mention the torrent of beautiful commemoratives and special issues which change at frequent intervals.

Business mail often yields a far wider selection, with the occasional foreign high values from registered and airmail packages or parcels. The cheapest source of supply is family and business correspondence, and once the word gets around that you are a stamp collector it is amazing how many stamps you can pick up in this way. It would be feasible to put together a collection of sorts without spending any money (other than on albums, hinges and other accessories), merely by relying on the material accumulated in this way, but inevitably there would be annoying gaps – odd definitive denominations and probably half the values in most commemorative sets. These are the stamps you never encounter on your own mail because they prepay overseas rates or fairly obscure postal charges.

Buying stamps for a collection

Sooner or later you would be compelled to buy stamps. Philately, like charity, should begin at home. The great majority of definitive and commemorative stamps can be purchased from your local post office at the time of their issue, but for the more unusual material, such as some booklets that are normally issued only in a certain area, regional stamps and pictorial air letters, coil stamps, postage-due labels and PHQ cards, you may have to pay a visit to the philatelic counter located only in the largest post offices, or open an account with the philatelic bureau. This is also a useful method should you decide to collect the stamps of other countries. As you progress in the hobby you will undoubtedly make use also of dealers and auctioneers. All of those methods of acquiring stamps are discussed more fully later in this book.

Mixed packets and kiloware

Many beginners get a tremendous boost to their collection by acquiring a bumper mixed packet of stamps, perhaps as a birthday or Christmas present. Packets of mixed stamps may be purchased from most stationers and department stores and average 100–1000 stamps. Some dealers specialize in this field and can offer packets with up to 100,000 different stamps – which would be guaranteed to put most collectors right off the hobby! Once you become a more advanced collector, specializing in the stamps of a single country, a useful source of material in bulk is kiloware. This term originally meant officially sealed parcels, weighing a kilogram, which were sold by some European postal administrations. The stamps in these kilo bags consisted mainly of high denominations clipped from parcel cards and commemoratives cut from unsold first-day covers. The term is now more widely used for any mixtures of stamps on paper, sold by weight. At one time these mixtures were described as 'bank' (mainly commercial) and 'mission' (collected by charities). Today everyone seems to be saving their stamps for some charity or other and vast quantities of stamps that might otherwise have been thrown away are now saved for posterity. Much of this material is sold by the charities to dealers for export and ends up in the cheap packets sold by stationers and department stores around the world; much of the 'packet trade' in Britain depends on imports of charity mixtures from abroad and there are dealers who sell nothing but such mixtures. Kiloware tends to be more carefully graded these days, so that you can buy a cheap mix (mainly low-denomination definitives), a special definitive mix (all values), large-sized pictorials only, or all-commemorative mixtures. Of course, you tend to accumulate a great many examples of the same stamp, but these mixtures, particularly the single-country lots, are ideal to the specialist who requires material in bulk for studying shades, perforations, minor printing flaws and the other minutiae of advanced philately. Kiloware is also an excellent source of supply for the collector looking for postmarks, especially from countries where a sizeable proportion of the mail continues to be hand-cancelled.

Kiloware – used stamps on paper

Floating the stamps off their backing paper and placing them face down on clean white blotting paper to dry

Removing stamps from covers

When begging for stamps from friends and relatives it is best to acquire them intact on the envelope or card if possible. This is because there might well be an interesting postmark on the cover, in which case no attempt should be made to remove the stamp from it. All too often well-meaning friends damage stamps by trying to get them off their covers by steaming or by peeling. Stamps forcibly wrenched from their covers usually leave some trace of themselves behind on the envelope – and a thinned stamp is virtually useless. Steaming a stamp off a cover can cause the gum to filter right through the paper and give the stamp a translucent 'oiled-paper' appearance or otherwise stain it. There is also a tendency by non-collectors to clip stamps off mail too closely for comfort, and this results in stamps with their perforations trimmed or cut into.

When you have decided to remove stamps from their covers you can cut out the backing paper carefully so as not to damage the stamp. The pieces can then be *floated* (never soaked) in a basin of lukewarm water, face upwards, until they part from the adhering paper easily. So many stamps these days are printed on very glossy paper, with fugitive inks and phosphor bands (discussed later on), that their appearance may be spoiled as a result of total immersion. When the stamps have been removed from their backing paper they can be laid flat between sheets of clean white blotting paper to dry, and then pressed flat under two or three books.

Condition and appearance of stamps

What you collect is entirely a matter for personal preference, but remember that if your collection is to have any value you will get into the habit early on of rejecting stamps that are less than perfect – though if the stamp is very rare and you are unlikely to get another example the rules can be relaxed a little. The blemishes that detract from a stamp's condition and appearance are heavy postmarks (unless, of course, you are collecting postmarks), thins, tears or holes, clipped or missing perforations, creases, surface rubbing, fading and water stains where fugitive colours have run. Such imperfections as foxing (rust spots) and oxidization (which can change the colour of a Penny Red till it almost resembles a Penny Black) can be removed by the judicious application of substances like chloramine-T and bleaching agents respectively, but these are highly skilled processes and best left to the experts. Stamps should also be well centred: imperforate stamps should have clear margins on all four sides, and perforated stamps should ideally be symmetrical, without any perforations close to or cutting into the design; but it is well-nigh impossible to find many of the older stamps in such ideal condition and you may have to be content with second best. Stamps perforated with firms' initials used to be rejected, but these 'perfins' are now avidly studied.

11 Albums and accessories

A century ago when stamp collecting was still in its infancy, the budding philatelist required no more than a school exercise book and a paste pot to begin housing his treasures. From time to time one of these primitive collections turns up and a hideous mess it looks! Nowadays collectors approach the hobby more systematically and have a much greater respect for their stamps. Having prepared your stamps by removing the backing paper, old hinges, etc. and sorted them into country order, you obviously want to put them somewhere safe and where you can examine them easily. Of course exercise books *can* be used, but stamp albums are so easy to obtain that it seems logical to start off correctly.

Many beginners start with a stamp collector's outfit: a package containing an album, stamp hinges and other accessories, and perhaps a booklet containing basic hints and a glossary of inscriptions which will aid identification. Some postal administrations even produce starter kits to encourage young people to take up a most satisfying and rewarding hobby and these follow a similar pattern.

There is such a bewildering array of albums available that some guidance is necessary. The beginner is advised to start with a fairly modest album, the usual type having fixed pages with printed headings and perhaps a few stamps illustrated, partly for decoration and partly to assist in identifying typical examples from each country. These printed albums often include hints for beginners and these notes are always worth studying. Many of the older albums were handsomely bound with die-struck pictorial covers, and the spacious headings reflected a more leisurely age. Portraits of rulers, national coats of arms, flags and crests adorned the headings, with a mass of statistical information about the country concerned. Nowadays, with the tremendous increase in the number of stamp-issuing countries, extraneous detail has to be kept to the minimum.

One of the drawbacks about fixed-leaf albums is that both sides of the page are meant to be used, and this can cause stamps to rip each others' perforations as the pages are turned over. Moreover, the collector soon finds that his stamps (particularly from the more important countries) outgrow their accommodation. He can then graduate to a loose-leaf album and there are many varieties with printed page headings, thereby combining the advantages of the fixed-leaf type without restricting the growth of the collection. Additional pages can be purchased with blank headings, and these can be inserted in the albums as and where they are required. Loose-leaf albums operate on various principles. The spring-back is useful if you want to insert fresh leaves without having to dismantle the binder.

A major disadvantage of this system is that the albums do not lie flat when opened, and if too many pages are inserted the springs get weakened and then the leaves slither around – to the detriment of the stamps.

Peg-fitting albums have the decided advantage that they lie flat when opened, and because the pages are held securely by the pegs there is no danger of their being dislodged. The main disadvantage is that if you wish to insert a new page you have to unpeg the binder and remove all the leaves up to the required place. The task of replacing the leaves correctly on their pegs tends to be somewhat tedious. The solution to this problem lies in the various types of multi-ring binders which enable the album to lie flat when open but facilitate the replacement or addition of pages by means of the patent catch.

Global and one-country albums

The Victorians developed a range of luxury albums with spaces printed for every stamp then issued. This idea survives to this day – the American Minkus Global and Master-Global albums are aimed at the whole-world collector – but I must confess that I find such mammoth albums difficult to handle, and even a large collection can look lost within these formidable pages. There are, however, many systems of one-country albums that offer a convenient method of collecting stamps, country by country, without the trouble of writing up the album pages. Many of these albums even have pictures of the stamps printed on the appropriate spaces so the task of arranging your stamps is greatly simplified. Mounting pairs, strips and blocks of stamps is a problem, since these albums only allow for single examples, but you can usually buy matching blank pages to fit these binders and they can be used for mounting covers as well. One-country albums are published by Stanley Gibbons and Collecta (Great Britain); Minkus and Scott (U.S.A.); Schaubek, Ka-Be, Lindner and Michel (Germany); and Yvert (France). Between them they cover every country in the world.

One-country albums, containing printed pages with spaces for every stamp

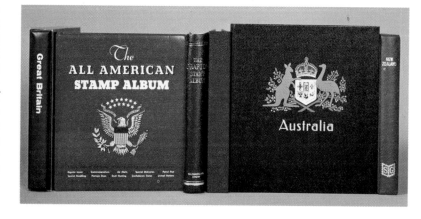

The more advanced collector prefers to use albums with blank pages on which he can arrange and annotate his stamps as he pleases. The pages have a feint pattern of tiny squares, rather like graph paper, so that it is possible to get the rows of stamps perfectly aligned. These are the album pages favoured for exhibition purposes, with or without glassine protective sheets, linen or paper hinges or rice-paper backing. There are also special albums for housing covers, booklets and miniature sheets.

Stamp hinges and other mounts

Next to the album the most important accessory is the stamp hinge or other form of mount. Hinges are made of very thin, strong, transparent paper, double-gummed for easy peeling so that they can be removed, if required, without damaging either the stamp or the album page. Never improvise with stamp edging or gummed paper. Adhesive tape, though admirable for sealing parcels, should never be used for sticking stamps in albums as the rubber fixative stains paper and will ruin both page and stamps. Hinges often seem very fiddly to use, but it takes little practice to master the art. Place the stamp face downwards, take the hinge and, if not already folded, fold it into a third and two-thirds with the gummed side outwards. Moisten the lesser portion and attach it lightly to the upper part of

when it comes to annotating the pages. The solution lies in the use of special strips with an adhesive backing and a transparent 'window'. The stamp is placed inside the strip which can then be affixed to the page. Strips come in numerous sizes tailored to suit every type of stamp and they greatly enhance the appearance of stamps as well as totally protecting them.

Handling stamps

Stamps should never be handled with the fingers since even the cleanest hands have a tiny film of grease or perspiration which can result in fingerprints adhering to the surface. For this purpose special tongs or tweezers (to use the American and British terms respectively) have been developed and can be purchased from most stamp dealers. They have flattened 'spade' ends which make the handling of stamps extremely easy.

For the examination of stamps in great detail some form of magnifier is necessary. Ordinary reading glasses are virtually useless, but again stamp dealers stock a wide range of special glasses of high magnification, many of them with built-in illumination. Other accessories which the more advanced collector will need include a good transparent ruler with a half-millimetre scale, callipers for measuring overprints, a perforation gauge, watermark detector and an ultra-violet quartz lamp.

right **The correct way to hinge stamps**

far right **The right way to hold stamps with tweezers or tongs**

below right **A selection of magnifiers including pocket and table models**

the back of the stamp, close to but not protruding beyond the perforations. Now moisten the other part of the hinge near the bottom end and attach stamp and hinge to the appropriate place on the page. Hinged stamps should lie perfectly flat, but they can be gently raised without difficulty to examine the backs if need be.

In recent years a fashion for unmounted mint stamps has developed and this has encouraged the growth of special hingeless albums or stock books, with transparent strips into which the stamps can be inserted. These albums are ideally suited for arranging stamps before giving them a permanent home, but they are very restrictive

12 The anatomy of a stamp

The beginner quickly realizes that stamps which often look the same are actually quite different and that such distinctions may greatly affect their value. Of course, there are many who prefer the simple life and are perfectly content to collect one of every design and denomination according to the Stanley Gibbons *Stamps of the World* catalogue, which does not bother with different types of paper, watermarks, perforations and other subtleties. Most collectors, however, develop a keen interest in certain issues and explore the minutiae that may make all the difference between a common (and very cheap) stamp and a major rarity worth a great deal of money. A good example of this is provided by the British halfpenny stamp, issued in 1971 and still current. The normal version has two vertical phosphor bands (sheets) or a single central band (coils and booklets) and both versions are very cheap. In 1972, however, a booklet was issued in honour of the Wedgwood pottery and contained on one pane ½p and 2½p stamps arranged in such a way that one halfpenny stamp had a single phosphor band at the left only. This stamp is very scarce and had a value in 1980 of £18 mint and £12 used. The ability to recognize this elusive item among similar but very common stamps is the sort of thing that comes with experience.

Apart from the different processes used to produce stamps, discussed in the next section, there are five aspects of modern stamps that may differ at some time or another during their currency and make for quite different collectable varieties. These are colour, paper, watermark or some other security device, perforations and electronic markings.

Colour

The most readily detected difference is the colour, since stamps produced over many years may run to numerous printings and in each case the printer would be unconcerned about using ink of the required shade and composition. Different shades or tints enable the specialist to place stamps in chronological order of production, and as some shades may be scarcer than others the value can be affected. Even in these modern times of frequent changes of definitives and more precise colour matching, shades inevitably occur.

Paper

Less apparent are the different types of paper that may be employed and quite an interesting collection could be formed to illustrate the range of papers which have been used for stamps. Among the kinds of paper would be sugar-bag paper (British Guiana); rice paper (Japan); newspaper (Jersey); goldbeater's skin (German high values of the 1870s); and transparent paper

(Saxony, 1946). Latvia's first stamps were printed on the backs of German military maps, incomplete Bolshevik and White Russian banknotes and paper torn from school exercise books, all of which can be identified by looking at the backs of the stamps. Paper can vary in type and quality from the expensive handmade rag paper used for many of the classic line-engraved issues, to modern, machine-made paper, produced from vegetable fibres and with a high kaolin content which gives it the smooth, glossy surface necessary for modern multicolour photogravure printing.

Many of the stamps printed by De La Rue for Britain and her colonies at the turn of the century were printed on ordinary or on chalk-surfaced paper. Apart from the fact that this constitutes two separate collectable versions it is necessary to be able to identify the chalk-surfaced paper, since stamps printed on it are more liable to suffer damage if immersed in water. A handy gadget obtainable from stamp dealers is a chalk pencil (with a silver tip which makes a black mark on chalk-surfaced paper but no mark on ordinary paper), though the edge of a silver (not cupronickel) coin will also do the trick.

Other kinds of paper which the collector will quickly learn to recognize include wove and laid (according to the mesh of the paper); granite paper (with bits of coloured fibre); *bleuté* or blued paper, caused by prussiate of potash in the printing ink; Dickinson paper, with a silk thread embedded in it; *batonné* paper, with feint lines ruled on it; and *quadrillé* paper with a pattern of squares, rather like graph paper. Tinted paper of various colours was used for many of the colonial stamps, but shortly before the First World War the printers had difficulties getting the right paper and thus the collector may find emergency printings on paper with a tinted front and a white back. Paper may range from pelure (very hard and thin) to cartridge (soft and thick); and in each case these differences may greatly affect the value of apparently identical stamps.

British 8p stamps used in 1979–80. *Left:* by Enschedé en Zonen of Haarlem; *right:* by Harrison & Sons, High Wycombe, distinguished by the Jubilee lines in the bottom margin and small cylinder number (61%)

Security devices

The commonest kind of security device is the watermark, a device that can usually be seen when the stamp is held up to the light, or is examined on the back at an oblique angle. More difficult cases may be detected by means of illuminated gadgets or special trays in which the stamp has a drop of benzine applied to the reverse. This makes it momentarily transparent, when the watermark can be seen against the black tray. Watermarks are impregnated into the paper when the pulp is rolled out. The sheets are squeezed under a roller, known as a dandy roll, made of wire gauze to which is attached the watermark bits – usually made of brass in various shapes and sizes. These bits make the paper slightly thinner at that point, hence their visibility when held to the light. The earliest British stamps had simple watermarks, a single device such as a crown, a garter or a star appearing on each stamp. Later on, however, multiple watermarks were adopted so that each stamp might have portions of several devices. British colonial stamps, for example, began with a star watermark, but later this was changed to a crown over CC (Crown Colonies) and then a crown over CA (Crown Agents). Early this century this changed to Multiple Crown CA and later still to Multiple Crown and Script CA, then Block CA and ultimately Spiral CA. British Elizabethan stamps had a watermark of the Royal cipher E 2 R surmounted by a Tudor crown (1952–4), followed by the same device but with a looped St Edward crown (1955–8), and then the E 2 R cipher was dropped in 1958 and a watermark of multiple crowns was substituted. Finally the watermark was withdrawn in 1967–8 and the 'Castles' high values and some of the regional stamps may be found in this version. Other countries have gradually abandoned the use of watermarks too, and this gives rise to watermarked and unwatermarked versions of otherwise identical stamps. Coils and booklets may be found with the watermark sideways or inverted, or the sheet of paper was the wrong way up when the stamps were being printed and the watermark may therefore be reversed.

Apart from the watermark, security devices may take the form of embedded silk threads of different colours (early Swiss stamps), grilles (classic American issues), and even imitation 'watermarks' printed on the back of the stamp under the gum (Greece, New Zealand, Sweden). Some countries had serial numbers on the reverse. Quite a number of stamps in recent years have had writing on the reverse of their stamps – either an overall pattern (Portugal) or giving a caption to the stamp design (United States, Portugal, Gibraltar, etc.).

Perforations

The earliest stamps were issued without perforations (i.e. imperforate) but from 1854 onwards this became the normal method of separation.

A Gibraltar stamp shaped like the silhouette of the Rock (150%)

The French philatelist Dr J. A. Legrand invented the *odontomètre* or perforation gauge which, in effect, counted the number of holes in a length of 2 centimetres. By laying a stamp alongside a series of black dots of differing sizes and spacing its perforation can be gauged. This is by far the commonest factor in creating differences between stamps and it is important to be able to measure perforations accurately and distinguish between line and comb or harrow perforations. Perforations actually remove tiny circles of paper, whereas rouletting merely pierces or cuts the paper, either in a straight line or in various fancy patterns, such as serpentine, arc or saw-tooth. Stamps with missing perforations between adjoining stamps are highly regarded errors, but stamps with straight edges may be from coils or booklets and may be worth no more than stamps with perforations on all four sides from sheets.

Electronic markings

For detecting differences in the composition of paper and printing ink an ultra-violet 'quartz' lamp is extremely useful, although its main function these days is to assist in distinguishing stamps with different types of fluorescence or phosphorescence. Phosphor bands, applied in vertical or horizontal bands across the face of a stamp, have been used by Britain and France in connection with the electronic sorting of mail. In Britain, for example, stamps for first-class mail have two bands, those for second-class mail have only one band. Since the 10p stamp was once the first-class stamp it originally appeared with two bands, but at the time of writing it has been re-issued with a single band for second-class mail. Conversely the 8p (formerly a single-band stamp for second-class mail) may be reissued with two bands since it can be used with a 4p stamp for first-class letters.

Britain has also used all-over phosphorescence and this system has been adopted by a number of other countries. Then there are stamps in which the phosphor element is in the printing ink or the paper itself, and in those instances the phosphorescence or fluorescence can only be detected with the quartz lamp. This lamp will also detect repairs to thins or tears, or the removal of a fiscal pen cancellation and the substitution of a faked postmark, since the original will show up under the ultra-violet rays.

13 Printing processes

Since the introduction of adhesive postage stamps five major processes have been used in printing, and since there are many cases in which two or more different methods have been used at various times during the currency of a series it is important to be able to distinguish them.

Intaglio printing

The earliest method used was called intaglio, copperplate or recess printing. The term line engraving is also rather loosely used, but should strictly apply only to the die or the plate from which the stamps are printed. In this process lines, grooves and recesses bite into the surface of the plate. Ink is then forced into these recesses and the surface of the plate wiped clean and hand polished. The paper is then forced under great pressure into the recesses where it absorbs the ink lying there. This gives the paper of such stamps its characteristic ridged surface. Most banknotes are produced by this process, hence their crisp surface where the timy ridges can be felt with the fingertips. This process was used for the British low values till 1880 and for the high values from 1913 to 1977. Until recently all American stamps were recess-printed and it is still used for most definitives. Canada, Austria, Czechoslovakia, France, Denmark and Sweden continue to use this process extensively, though elsewhere it has been largely superseded by cheaper processes.

Letterpress printing

Letterpress, relief or surface printing is sometimes known by philatelists as typography and stamps by this method are said to be 'typographed'. This process is the opposite to intaglio, since the surface of the plate is cut away leaving ridges on which the ink is spread. The paper is pressed against the raised lines of the plate and picks up the image from them. The chief merit of this method was the cheapness with which printing blocks, clichés or stereos, could be cast, but it was incapable of producing such fine and sensitive results as intaglio. The lines were always much coarser and tended to clog up with ink thus producing a rather blurred effect. This method was used by De La Rue to print British stamps from 1854 onwards (exclusively from 1880 till 1913) and many of the colonial issues as well. The low values continued to be produced by this method till 1934 and the postage-dues till 1970. Irish stamps were surface-printed until 1966 when photogravure (see below) was used for a fairly short-lived version of the 3d and 5d stamps which are consequently worth much more than the letterpress version. Variants of letterpress include typesetting, in which stamp designs were composed from loose type and printers' ornament (early British Guiana, and

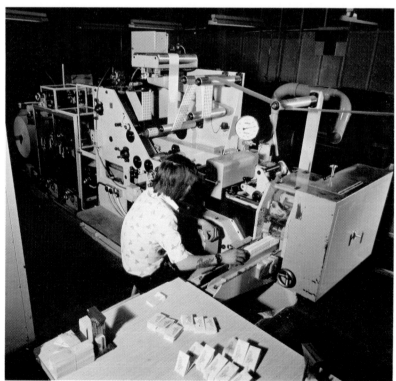

the first issues of Fiji, Lithuania and Uganda), and half-tone, a process used for reproducing photographs in newspapers and periodicals (Indian states such as Kishangarh and Orchha). A characteristic of letterpress printing is the slight indentations visible on the backs of the stamp itself.

Lithography

This telltale indentation is absent in the process known as lithography, which is often confused with letterpress. It is an entirely flat process which relies on the fact that grease repels water. It derives its name (from Greek *lithos*, 'stone', and *graphein* – 'to write') from the fact that slabs of finely polished limestone were used in the printing. It was a German actor named Alois Senefelder who discovered, about 1795, that the yellowish-grey limestone from the Solenhofen quarries near Munich could be polished to a very smooth surface and that a drawing made on it with a substance known as fat ink could be used to print impressions on paper. The stone would be wetted and a roller inked over the stone. The fat ink on the roller would be repelled by the wetted portion of the stone, but taken up by the fat ink impression of the drawing. The paper placed over the stone would then take up an impression from the inked area. Various methods of transferring a stamp design in multiples to the lithographic stone were evolved and the process was adapted for stamp production. Occasionally, however, the design was applied directly by hand straight on to the stone, as, for example, the primitive design by Sergeant Triquerat which was used for the Napoleon stamps of New Caledonia in 1860. Though actual

limestone is used to this day other processes have been developed on the same principle, using lightweight sheets of zinc instead. A kind of lithography used in the 1930s was known as photo-zincography, but in more recent years off-set lithography has been used increasingly. In this process the design is not printed direct from the plate but is transferred to a rubber roller which then comes in contact with the printing surface. Refinements of this often go under various trade names, such as Delacryl (used by De La Rue) and Duotone (used by the Canadian Bank Note Co.). Lithography is nowadays combined with intaglio to create startling multicolour effects, retaining the incisive quality associated with recess printing.

Embossing

This technique was introduced for the postal stationery issued by Britain in 1841 and continues to be used for the stamps printed on registered and ordinary envelopes. It is also widely used by many other countries in their postal stationery, but is much less common in adhesive stamps. The earliest British 6d, 10d and 1s stamps were thus printed, as were many Swiss stamps till 1882; the Arms stamps of the German Empire (1872–5) and Bavaria (1867–1911); the so-called Cameos of the Gambia; most of the stamps of Heligoland; and the early stamps of Austrian Italy and Portugal. It is very seldom used nowadays, though several West German commemoratives since 1953 have made effective use of colourless embossing on a coloured background. The Queen's profile has been embossed in gold foil on various British and Commonwealth commemoratives since 1967. Stamps

opposite **Taking up the soft steel transfer roll from the hardened steel original die**

left **Machine printing the covers of British stamp booklets and making up the booklets with pre-printed stamps**

right **Embossed stamps from the Gambia, Heligoland, Bavaria, Sardinia, West Germany and Portugal** (161%)

left The engraver repairing a photogravure cylinder for faults

below A detail of the highly sophisticated Jumelle press used for photogravure and intaglio printing of stamps

actually embossed entirely on metal foil were pioneered by Tonga in 1963 and since then Sierra Leone, Bhutan, Burundi, Qatar and some countries of the French Community have issued metal-embossed stamps, many of them being circular or free-form with self-adhesive backing.

Photogravure

The most widely used process at the present day is photogravure – cheap, efficient and technically versatile since it is capable of the most subtle and complex multicolour reproduction. Known also as heliogravure and rotogravure it was first used philatelically in 1914 for the production of Bavarian definitives. Harrison and Sons were the first of the British stamp printers to recognize its potential and they printed stamps by this process for Egypt (1923) and the Gold Coast (1928) before changing the British low-value definitives from letterpress to photogravure in 1934. As the name suggests, it relies heavily on photography, and is to intaglio what half-tone is to letterpress. A photogravure plate or cylinder bears a photographic image etched into its surface. The ink goes into the recesses which, in this case, are composed of fine dots of varying density, and the paper picks up the impression in much the same manner as in intaglio. Under a magnifying glass you can see the fine patterns of dots which are always present in photogravure. A screening process is also used in half-tone and in modern offset lithography and it is not always possible to tell them apart, though photogravure

generally has greater depth and tonal qualities than the others and is capable of much finer results.

Marginal markings

Associated with the various processes are the markings to be found in the margins of stamps. Jubilee lines and 'pillars' of fine horizontal lines were used as reinforcements in letterpress plates and may be found on sheet margins and gutters. Jubilee lines are also found on photogravure stamps by Harrisons and this is virtually the only way of distinguishing Harrison's British 8p stamps from those printed in 1979 in Holland by Enschedé of Haarlem. Cylinder and plate numbers in one or more corners identify the cylinders and plates used in production, while colour dabs or 'traffic lights' are marginal markings associated with multicolour photogravure and offset lithography. Changes of contractor may be reflected in marginal inscriptions on sheets of prewar Australian stamps, or in colonial issues in the 1960s when the Waterlow contracts were taken over by De La Rue. Some countries use the sheet margins to indicate the total value of the row; others have used this space for commercial advertising, and Israel, for example, uses it for explanatory tabs.

A miniature sheet produced for the 1980 International Stamp Exhibition at Earl's Court showing the separate colour printings that go into making a stamp (150%)

14 General collecting

Everyone starts off with a general collection, containing everything and anything that remotely resembles a stamp. Gradually, as knowledge and discernment improve, the non-philatelic items get weeded out. Collectors of not so long ago would have discarded labels, stationery cut-outs, local stamps, revenue and telegraph stamps and even perfins, but nowadays each of these subjects has a steady following and it is wiser to form a sideline collection, such as those described under the heading of Cinderella Philately (p. 58), or to put such items aside for exchange.

If you decide to pursue general collecting you may feel that government-issued adhesive postage stamps, which are listed in the standard stamp catalogues, are a vast enough subject without delving into any of the murky depths of sideline material. One thing you may be certain of: even if you have unlimited money at your disposal you are never going to form a complete collection of all the stamps of the world. Even on a simplified basis, ignoring variations in shade, watermark, perforation, gum, phosphorescence and printing process, the number of different stamps which have appeared since 1840 is now well in excess of 200,000 and these range in value from the ten-a-penny issues to unique rarities like the British Guiana One Cent Black on Magenta, which was sold in April 1980 for the record sum of £445,000. With new issues appearing at the present rate of 6000–7000 every year the task of keeping such a collection up to date would be daunting, and the job of acquiring all the obsolete stamps well-nigh impossible.

There is no denying the pleasure that can be gained from general collecting. There are many philatelists of long standing, eminent authorities on some specialized aspect or other, who keep a general collection going. It has been said, with some measure of truth, that a specialist is someone who knows more and more about less and less, and ultimately knows everything about nothing. You can keep a proper perspective on the hobby, and not get too obsessive about one specific area, by making a general collection. There are also many collectors who regard themselves as specialists because they have narrowed down their interests to a single country or a group of countries, but in reality they are merely general collectors with a limited scope. Completeness is one of the bugbears of philately and even on a general, simplified basis you have to set some limits if anything like a comprehensive, far less a complete, collection is to be formed.

Narrowing the field

If the whole world is too much, and a single country too restrictive, the answer lies somewhere in the middle. Twenty years ago most general collectors would have attempted to collect the stamps of the British Commonwealth as a whole. At that time definitives were changed once a decade and commemoratives were issued very sparingly. Today definitives change at least every five years, and often more frequently, while commemoratives are produced at the rate of six sets a year on average, even by the smallest colony which resorts to publicizing international events for lack of anniversaries and events of its own to celebrate. Consequently the Commonwealth has become too unwieldy a group for all but the wealthiest, and this area has tended to be divided into more compact groups.

The most popular field for British collectors nowadays is the United Kingdom, the 'offshore islands' – Guernsey, Jersey and the Isle of Man – and, to a growing extent, the Irish Republic, since these are the five independent postal administrations located in the British Isles. Even collecting the stamps of these five countries on a simplified basis, e.g. single sets of mint stamps and first-day covers, would cost in excess of £50 a year, or a pound a week. Australians collect the stamps of their own country first and foremost, and include the issues of Australian Antarctica, Norfolk Island, Christmas Island, the Cocos-Keeling Islands and the republic of Nauru, which has close ties with Australia. Similarly

A selection of Elizabethan definitive stamps from the Commonwealth, ranging from simple portrait designs to multicolour pictorials (61%)

New Zealanders tend to concentrate nowadays on New Zealand, Ross Dependency, Tokelau Islands, and the independent countries of Western Samoa, the Cook Islands (including the issues by Aitutaki and Penrhyn) and Niue, for the same reasons. South Africans collect their own stamps as well as those of South West Africa (Namibia), the three 'Bantustans' of Transkei, Bophuthatswana and Venda, and perhaps also the issues of Botswana, Lesotho and Swaziland (the former High Commission territories within or neighbouring South Africa) and probably Rhodesia (Zimbabwe) as well. Americans and Canadians collect each other's stamps and both also have a strong predilection for the stamps of the Caribbean islands. Political and geographical groupings of this sort may be found in every part of the world and collecting along those lines is both practical and manageable.

An alternative form of general collecting is to concentrate on one of the larger countries and attempt to form a general collection of its stamps right back to the very first issue. Many so-called specialists are, in fact, no more than general collectors of a single country. Even on a simplified basis it would take a great deal of time and money to put together general collections of Britain, the United States, France or Germany, but many people have done it and these collections then become the nucleus for something more advanced.

As an alternative to regional or country collecting, many philatelists prefer to study the stamps of a single reign. Elizabethan stamps are the most popular in this group and those collectors who began modestly enough in 1953 with the Coronation omnibus series and have managed to stick with it will now have collections running to many albums. For the newcomer to philately, Elizabethan stamps as a whole present a very daunting prospect. This explains the increased popularity of the stamps issued in the reign of King George VI (1936–52), a period in which the collector has a better chance of attaining completion. Similarly there has been renewed interest in the Edwardian issues which first appeared in 1902 and continued in some colonies till the First World War.

Obsolete stamps

The one advantage of concentrating on obsolete stamps is that the subject is finite, unlike modern issues which are open-ended. At one time there was little interest in the 'dead countries' – those that had ceased to issue their own stamps, but in recent years they have swung back into favour. Germans naturally concentrate on the issues of the kingdoms, principalities and duchies that issued their own stamps from 1849 till 1871, with Bavaria and Württemberg continuing as late as 1920. Italians favour the stamps issued by the various states before the country was unified in the 1860s, though this is a much harder field to cover then the German issues. The six Australian states – New South Wales, Queensland, South Australia, Tasmania (originally known as Van Diemen's Land), Victoria and Western Australia – issued their own stamps from the 1850s till 1913, and as many of these stamps are still inexpensive this is a popular field with Australian philatelists. Similarly Canadians collect the issues of New Brunswick, Newfoundland, Nova Scotia, Prince Edward Island, British Colombia and Vancouver Island and South Africans favour the stamps of Cape of Good Hope, Natal, the Orange Free State and the Transvaal, plus the more ephemeral countries like Griqualand West, Zululand, British Bechuanaland, Stellaland and the New Republic.

The supranationals

An interesting group consists of the United Nations, which has issued its own stamps in New York since 1951, in Geneva since 1969 and in Vienna since 1979. In addition, the Swiss postal administration produced distinctive stamps for the League of Nations from 1922 to 1944 and for the United Nations from 1950 to 1969, as well as separate issues for eight other international agencies, such as the International Labour Office, the World Health Organization and the International Education Office. The UN also had its own stamps at the Brussels Fair (1958) and the Montreal Expo (1967). This is an immensely popular group that transcends national boundaries and political outlook.

Since 1950 special stamps have been provided for the use of delegates and officials of the Council of Europe in Strasbourg. Since 1960 they have also been available to visitors to the Council headquarters. Distinctive stamps are also issued at UNESCO headquarters in Paris (since 1961) and at the International Court of Justice in The Hague (since 1934).

United Nations stamps issued for use in New York, Geneva, Montreal and Vienna (63%)

15 Thematic collecting

Whether general or specialized, stamp collecting traditionally followed set lines. Stamps were collected and mounted in albums according to their country and date of issue, and this is the pattern followed by the great majority of stamp catalogues, which are designed to help the collector put his material in the correct order. In an age when definitive stamps were small in size and conservative in design, and commemoratives were few or non-existent, there was not much scope for the collector to arrange his stamps by any other system, although a few unorthodox and imaginative people did attempt to arrange their stamps according to their subject – portraits of rulers, portraits of famous men and women in history, coats of arms and allegory. The more unashamedly pictorial approach of the Seebeck issues at the turn of the century, and particularly the spate of stamps honouring Columbus and his exploits in the New World, encouraged philatelists to form sideline collections arranged by motif. By 1900, for example, stamps featuring locomotives had been issued by the United States, New Brunswick, the Transvaal and quite a few Latin American countries, and if you included the stamps of the private local posts that flourished on both sides of the Atlantic, plus the various railway letter and parcel stamps, it was possible to form quite an attractive collection with a railway theme.

By the 1920s there were so many more stamps available, and the tendency towards greater pictorialism was well established. In addition to the old favourites, such as portraiture and heraldry, ships, railways and maps were popular themes, to which could be added stamps depicting aircraft as commercial aviation rapidly developed. It should be noted that many of the stamps of this period showing aircraft were not intended for airmail. Often enough the issue of a stamp featuring a plane was merely wishful thinking on the part of a government which had not yet the means of instituting an airmail service. Even then, stamps were regarded as something of a status symbol or an image builder and many countries were not slow in appreciating the propaganda value of attractive pictorial designs.

Nevertheless, people who admitted to collecting stamps according to their subject were regarded as eccentric to say the least, but after the Second World War it gradually became more acceptable and even acquired distinctive names – *Motiv-Sammlung* in Germany, thematic collecting in Britain, and topical collecting in America. In 1949 the American Topical Collectors' Association was formed and today the ATA has almost 10,000 members in over 80 different countries. It has helped to make topical or thematic collecting easier by publishing numerous checklists of stamps depicting specific subjects, as well as annual summaries of stamps of the world according to their subject. This has developed in both America and Europe and there are now detailed and well-illustrated catalogues devoted to the more popular subjects such as fauna and flora, religion, fine art, space exploration, the Europa theme, the Red Cross, Boy Scouts and above all sport. At one time dealers were reluctant to break up sets so that the collector interested in a particular theme could purchase the one stamp he needed, but nowadays postal administrations are more thematically conscious and tend to issue entire sets, including definitives, with a single theme.

Perhaps it is all becoming *too* easy. In the 1960s my wife started collecting stamps showing stained-glass windows, and slowly and patiently she eventually acquired examples of every stamp that had ever depicted this unusual subject. A few years later, however, when many postal administrations had seemingly exhausted the wealth of Old Masters with religious themes for their annual Christmas and Easter stamps, they suddenly discovered stained glass and this led to a positive torrent of stamps with this theme. This is as nothing, however, compared with the deluge of stamps from every part of the world that greets each Olympiad. Nor is it necessary any longer to confine such stamps to the Olympic Games themselves. What with 'aftermath' issues by countries honouring their Olympic gold medallists, and 'pre-publicity' issues by the host for the next Olympiad and any other country that may or may not have a legitimate interest in the matter, there is no closed season for the Olympic theme. Even the collector who decides to limit his interests to a particular sport may find things getting out of hand, particularly if football is his chosen subject.

The increasing choice of themes

The combination of much more frequent issues and the use of modern multicolour printing processes has greatly widened the scope of stamp design and there is now hardly a subject under the sun that has not had stamps devoted to it. Even if collectors have become soured by the so-called bandwagon issues there is still plenty of material for them to explore. Ideally you want to find a subject that has not been overdone, but offers a reasonable amount of variety. Thematic collectors are becoming more and more selective in their choice. One collector, for example, has formed collections of stamps showing bicycles and umbrellas, and has even come across stamps that show both: one from Laos featuring a cycle rickshaw and a bystander carrying a parasol; and another from Russia portraying the writer Chekhov carrying an umbrella, with a bicycle just visible in the background.

A range of stamps illustrating the theme of stained-glass windows, including a *se-tenant* strip from Anguilla showing five different windows (63%)

pilots and truck drivers can collect stamps depicting aircraft and road vehicles. Others might collect stamps honouring the nursing profession or Mother's Day. Freemasons, rotarians, Esperantists, Boy Scouts and members of Lions' Clubs will all find a wealth of material of specific relevance to them. You may not be able to afford to collect Old Masters or Post-Impressionists, but you can have a most impressive picture gallery of your own, since every aspect of fine art from Stone Age cave paintings to Surrealism and Dadaism has been reproduced on stamps. Numismatists can combine an interest in coins and medals with stamps depicting them; collectors of militaria can form a sizeable collection of stamps depicting badges and insignia, uniforms and headdress, arms and armour and military equipment of all kinds. Sculpture, architecture, folk arts and crafts have all found adequate coverage in stamps. Even stamps themselves have frequently been reproduced, mainly in connection with the centenary or anniversary of first issues, but also to publicize stamp exhibitions. The centenary of the death of Sir Rowland Hill in 1979 was a marvellous opportunity for virtually every country to issue stamps in his honour and, at the same time, reproduce their own historic issues.

Subject collecting

Thematic or topical collecting can be divided into three broad categories, each of which has a large following and even has its own set of rules, at least so far as competitive exhibitions are concerned. Perhaps the most popular of these groups is known more specifically as subject collecting, since it consists of arranging stamps according to the subject depicted on them. If you decide to collect stamps depicting flowers, insects, wild animals, horses, poultry, jet aircraft or fairy-tale characters most of the hard work has already been done since the ATA has published handbooks on all of these topics. If, however, you are of a more independent frame of mind and spurn paths well-trodden by other collectors, you will have to start with the latest edition of a whole world stamp catalogue and wade you way through page after page, from Abu Dhabi to Zululand, making notes of all the stamps that seem to come within your scope. This will take you quite some time but it can be a most rewarding task since inevitably you will come across many interesting items and greatly increase your general knowledge of the geographical location of many smaller countries and states and the world's stamps in the process.

From the catalogue you will get the country and date of issue, the denomination of the stamp, whether it is a series or a single item, and a brief idea of the subject itself. You will end up with extensive lists of stamps, still in country order, and the next stage is to regroup the data so that your subject can be subdivided into its various aspects. Supposing you have decided to collect

Although purists of the old school still deride topical collecting as child's play there is no doubt that this has done more to recruit newcomers to the hobby than the more traditional methods. Just as the eye-catching and colourful designs of modern stamps have stimulated general interest, so also have exhibits devoted to particular subjects attracted attention and opened people's eyes to the potential of stamp collecting. Some public libraries now mount regular exhibitions of stamps devoted to various subjects and use this as the focal point for a display of books on these subjects. Many adults have taken up stamp collecting because of a link with their profession or other pursuits. Doctors and dentists can collect stamps with a medical theme, airline

stamps featuring horses. You would find that the subject can be broken down into the following groups:

Early history
Prehistoric horses, wild horses, horse relatives (zebras, asses and hybrids (mules)
Mythological horses, centaurs, Pegasus, etc.
Horses in folklore and legend
Medieval horses
War horses and chargers, knights on horseback
Related equestrian subjects in heraldry and applied art
Horse in literature – epic poems, novels
The horse in paintings, sculpture and other art forms
Horses and their uses
Work horses, plough horses
Horse-drawn coaches and other vehicles
Mail carried on horseback
Mounted police and cavalry
Horses used in hunting
Chariot racing, steeplechasing, flat racing, trotting
Polo, buzkashi, guks and other equestrian team games
Horses in bullfights, tournaments and circuses
Show jumping, dressage and haute école movements
Ancillary subjects
Saddlery and harness
Horse ploughs
Portraits of famous jockeys, race trophies

Stamps depicting horses have been issued by almost every country at some time or another. Some idea of the immensity of this theme can be gained from examining the stamps of a few countries, taken at random. From Australia, for example, come the following stamps:

1935 Silver Jubilee – three stamps showing King George V mounted on the horse Anzac'
1949 UPU 75th Anniversary – 3½d showing a mounted postman in the outback
1953 Produce Food – 3d and 3½d showing a stockman herding cattle
1955 Cobb & Co, mailcoach 3½d and 2s
1960 Northern Territory Centenary – 'The Overlanders', after Sir Daryl Lindsay
1960 100th Melbourne Cup Race – racehorse and jockey Fred Archer, 1861
1961 Definitive – 5s showing an Aboriginal stockman
1962 Blue Mountains 150th Anniversary – 5d showing an explorer leading his horse
1965 Gallipoli 50th Anniversary – Simpson and his donkey (three stamps)
1971 Animals – 6-cent showing a draught horse
1972 Olympic Games – 35-cent showing equestrianism
1972 Pioneer Life – 50-cent showing a stage coach

1974 Christmas – woodcut by Albrecht Dürer of the 'Flight into Egypt'
1978 Horseracing – four stamps showing famous horses

With the exception of the Produce Food stamps, where the stockman is tucked away in the background, each of these stamps shows horses quite prominently and usually as the primary subject. Thematic collectors, however, delight in finding their subjects in secondary positions or reduced to microscopic proportions, and they would certainly wish to include the set of three stamps issued in 1936 for the centenary of South Australia. The design shows Adelaide in 1836 and under the gum trees on the left the tiny figure of a man on horseback can just be made out.

Purpose-of-issue collecting

A more recent development in thematics has been purpose-of-issue collecting. In America this is sometimes known as incidental philately and denotes the collecting of stamps issued for a particular incident or event. The omnibus issues come into this category, but it is widened to include all stamps issued in connection with the same event, whether in omnibus sets or not. The stamps of 1892–8 honouring the discovery of America, and the stamps of 1897–8 celebrating Queen Victoria's Diamond Jubilee rank as the

left **An enlargement of the British intaglio 2s 6d Shakespeare, showing the fine engraving (154%)**

below **Some of the stamps issued in 1964 to celebrate the quatercentenary of William Shakespeare. The Bahamas stamp** *(top left)* **was one of a uniform omnibus series issued in twelve Commonwealth countries (66%)**

earliest issues which come under this heading. Since then there have been stamps for peace or victory after both world wars; the New York World's Fair (1939) and the postwar world fairs from Brussels (1958) to Osaka (1970); jubilees and anniversaries of the UPU (1949 and 1974), and Rotary International (1955 and 1980); the quatercentenary of Shakespeare (1964); and the centenaries of Winston Churchill (1974) and Rowland Hill (1979) among many others in recent years. In addition, the United Nations has designated annual events from World Refugee Year (1959–60) to International Year of

A selection of stamps issued in 1979 in honour of the International Year of the Child (66%)

the Child (1979) and these events have been widely commemorated by stamps. International Year of the Handicapped falls in 1981 and we may anticipate numerous issues with charity premiums. One drawback about such events is that interest tends to pall once their immediate topicality disappears. If, however, they are linked to a subject that continually inspires new stamps (such as Scouting, the Red Cross, Olympics or the Rotary movement) collections devoted to specific anniversaries can be integrated into the larger grouping.

Mourning stamps would come under the heading of a subject collection if they comprised all the stamps, from Abraham Lincoln's 17-cent stamp of 1866 to President Tito, issued in memory of famous men and women. Many of these stamps were printed in sombre hues, and there was a prewar fashion for giving such stamps a heavy black border, after the manner of the stationery used by people in mourning. Such stamps become a purpose-of-issue collection when they pertain exclusively to a single person, and this became possible in 1963–4 when numerous countries issued stamps in honour of John F. Kennedy. Subsequently Winston Churchill, Charles de Gaulle, Martin Luther King, Robert Kennedy, Eleanor Roosevelt and Konrad Adenauer were honoured in this way.

True thematics

The third branch of thematics offers the greatest scope to the collector and has been described as true thematics: the arrangement of stamps in such a way that they develop a theme or concept. In effect, the stamps are used to illustrate a story and tend to become merely incidental to the historical research undertaken by the collector. Among the more popular themes are the history of the United States as portrayed on its stamps, or (a prime favourite in Communist countries) 'Fascism no more', contrasting the evils and excesses of the Fascist era through the medium of Nazi German stamps, with liberty and democracy as reflected in modern stamps of the Soviet bloc. This theme is particularly popular in the German Democratic Republic, which has encouraged its development by issuing numerous anti-fascist sets and stamps commemorating the concentration camps of occupied Europe. Many stamps have a didactic element or political undertones and they can be used to express ideas most effectively. Far less controversial are such themes as 'Vision', with stamps tracing the history of optics and showing different kinds of spectacles, telescopes and microscopes, television, cinema and visual entertainment; or 'Man's Conquest of Space' as illustrated by stamps depicting rocketry from ancient China to the Apollo moon landings. The possibilities with this type of collection are endless and stamps can be, and are used, to illustrate everything from nuclear physics to Shakespeare quotations.

16 Postal history

Postal-history material embraces everything from Sumerian clay tablets of 3000 BC to the postcoded envelope retrieved from the office wastepaper basket this morning. It is a rather misleading term since postal services are constantly evolving and collectors have to be on the alert all the time for collectable material associated with the latest developments. Interest in the background to the postal services developed very slowly from the latter years of the nineteenth century. Until then – and, indeed, for many years thereafter – most philatelists preferred their stamps in mint condition and regarded a cancellation as an unsightly blemish, to be avoided at all costs. A few more discerning individuals, however, paid closer attention to the postmarks on their stamps and began to form small sideline collections of stamps on pieces of envelopes, bearing complete cancellations. Gradually this idea took hold and several notable collections devoted entirely to postmarks were formed in France, Germany, Britain and the United States in the early years of this century. Postmark collecting remained an esoteric subject till the 1950s when greater use of slogan cancellations attracted the attention of many philatelists. Up to that time it was considered sufficient to have the postmark on a cut-out piece of envelope or postcard, but since then collectors have shown a preference for entires, especially those that have other postmarks on them than mere cancellations.

Earlier sections of this book have shown how postal services were well organized long before the advent of adhesive stamps and it was to this period – often, though incorrectly, known as the 'stampless' or 'pre-stamp' period – that collectors turned when they graduated from being mere collectors of postmarks to postal historians. Strictly speaking you do not have to collect this material to be a postal historian, and there are many who are content to study aspects of postal history without actually collecting old letters, which are only one aspect of the subject. But for most people 'Postal history' has become synonymous with collecting covers and postcards for the sake of their postal markings, regardless of whether they then go on to study the historical background to their issue.

The first thing that the beginner discovers is that, compared with a straightforward stamp collection, postal history is infinitely more complex and a great deal bulkier. Even a collection of the postmarks of one country, on pieces clipped from kiloware, would rapidly fill an album, while a serious collection of a country's postal history, entailing thousands of entire letters, covers and postcards, might fill a room. Twenty years ago, particularly in Britain, old letters could be had by the sackful from wastepaper merchants and property developers as the attics and cellars of old legal and commercial businesses were cleared to make way for office redevelopment. Those were the happy days when collectors and dealers alike were largely ignorant of what were the rare postmarks, and pre-stamp entires were sold for 'fourpence each or four for a shilling', regardless of their age or postal markings. All this has changed within the past decade and not only is everyone much more knowledgeable, but the market has hardened very considerably, and there have been many instances of a single pre-stamp letter fetching thousands of pounds at auction.

Cancellations old and new

Like everything else in philately, however, postal history can be tailored to suit the pocket of the individual. By collecting the more interesting envelopes that come into your office or home you would soon build up quite a formidable collection at little or no cost at all, but this may be too haphazard and some definite plan should be adopted. A very popular field is slogan cancellations, now used in almost every country employing machines to cancel mail. Although slogans have their origin in the quaint hand-struck marks of London (1661–75) which proclaimed, 'The Post for all Kent goes every night from the Round House in Love Lane and comes every morn', or 'Essex Post goes and comes every day', the idea was not revived till the turn of the century and was then used as an alternative to the straight or wavy-line obliterators fitted to cancelling machines. Slogans were used in the United States, Canada and New Zealand in the early 1900s. Britain did not adopt them till 1917, when they were used to promote national savings and war bonds. For many years thereafter they were confined to public announcements, mainly concerned with early posting for Christmas or buying British goods. Some European countries, notably France and Germany, used slogans extensively to promote local tourism and this idea has since spread. Britain began using local publicity slogans in 1963, for both tourism and industry, and also to celebrate local events. This pattern is also used in the United States, Canada, Australia and New Zealand, though pictorialism is used much more sparingly.

Machine cancellations of the non-slogan variety date in their present form from the 1880s, though much earlier than that Pearson Hill (son of Sir Rowland) pioneered machine cancelling to speed up the handling of mail. When adhesive stamps were introduced it was necessary to cancel the adhesive with an obliterator (the Maltese Cross) and apply a datestamp to the reverse of the letter. In 1844 obliterators containing identifying numerals were adopted, and this idea, in various guises, spread to many other countries. In the 1850s the stamping process was streamlined by combining the numeral obliterator with the circular datestamp to form duplex stamps. In the 1880s the dating and obliterating elements were integrated to form so-called combined stamps, such as the 'squared circles' used in England, Italy, Canada and South Africa, and the double-circle stamps with obliterating arcs used in Scotland and Ireland. Double-circle stamps were modified and extended to England in the 1890s and have since been widely employed all over the world, though the 'killer' arcs have become substantially lighter and thinner since 1949. Many European countries preferred circular postmarks with patterns of vertical bars above and below the date. This 'bridge' type has also been considerably modified over the years but survives in a more streamlined form in Germany, Austria, Denmark and some other countries.

Postal mechanization since the Second World War has led to the introduction of postcodes (known in America as the zip code) and these may be found in both handstamps and machine cancellations. Germany, Norway, Austria and Italy use serials with up to four numbers, whereas the United States has five-figure numbers and Canada uses combinations of numbers and letters. Britain has the latter system but very few datestamps incorporate the codes. Belgium, Switzerland, India and Australia have recently incorporated their postcode numbers in their postmarks and other countries are following suit as they update their postmarks.

Cancellations are but a single aspect of postmarks, which include backstamps and transit marks, charge and explanatory marks, and a whole host of special marks applied to registered and late-fee mail, parcels and packets, and several important categories of mail that now enjoy a large following and are noted separately below. Though handstamping is rapidly dying out as mail handling is centralized and mechanized, it is still used for exhibitions and special events that have specially designed cancellations, often highly ornate in character. Isolated examples of these 'special event' handstamps are known from the 1880s, but they developed more rapidly after the First World War and are now very widely used. In addition, Germany, Austria, Switzerland, Belgium and Denmark use handstamps to publicize the tourist attractions of the smaller towns and villages. Pictorial postmarks of this type have been used sporadically in Britain, Sweden, India, Australia, South Africa and New Zealand.

First day of issue postmarks
Most countries now make special arrangements for the handling of mail posted on the first day of issue of each series of stamps and not only publish special first-day covers (popularly known as FDCs) but furnish distinctive postmarks inscribed 'First day of issue', or the equivalent in other languages, such as *Premier jour d'émission* (French), *Ersttagsbrief* (German), *Primo giorno dell'emisione* (Italian), *Eerste dag van uitgifte* (Dutch). The custom of sending oneself a set of stamps on the first day of issue began in America before the First World War on an unofficial basis, but by the 1920s special cachets or rubber stamps were often applied to the envelope. Later still came specially printed envelopes and by the time of the Second World War the custom was well enough established for the US Post Office to provide first-day facilities including special postmarks. The idea spread to Europe but it was not until 1964 that Britain introduced first-day postmarks, and then only at a few of the largest post offices. Nowadays this facility is offered by most of the head offices throughout the country. A similar procedure is followed almost everywhere else, both hand and machine cancellations being used.

Maximum cards
A somewhat similar craze is known as maximaphily, or the collecting of maximum cards. This arose from the picture-postcard mania at the turn of the century, when many collectors tried

First Day Cover of the New Zealand health *se-tenant* strip, 1977; First Day Cover of the Australian stamp marking the 50th Anniversary of Parliament House, Canberra. Note the use of pictorial vignettes and special handstamps in conjunction with the commemorative stamps

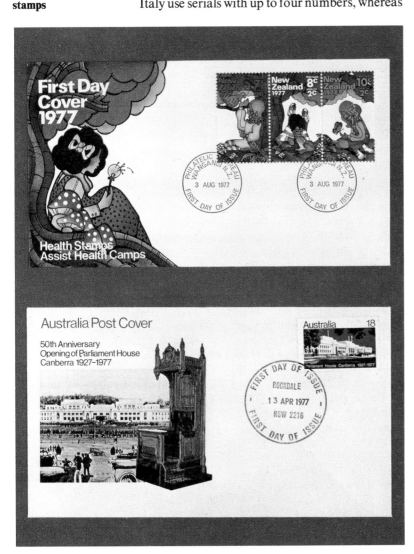

to match the picture with a postmark relevant to it, and even went so far as to stick the stamp on the picture side. The ideal maximum was a picture, postmark *and* stamp of related design and this became increasingly popular as stamps became more pictorial in concept. This practice was frowned on by many postal administrations and maximum cards have only been permitted in Britain since 1970: the PHQ cards previously mentioned are a form of spin-off from this practice.

Sea mails

The purist postal historian tends to look down on first-day covers, maximum cards and similar antics. He is more likely to be concerned with material that illustrates the methods by which mail was transported, or items sent through the post in times of war and international crises. Airmail has already been discussed, since it has resulted in such a large number of adhesive stamps, but earlier and more traditional forms of mail transportation have left their mark in the stamp album. Up to the mid-nineteenth century, and sometimes even later, mail arriving by private ship from abroad was treated as a ship letter, charged at a special rate that included a penny or twopence for the shipmaster. Many seaports round the British coast had special postmarks incorporating the words 'Ship letter', and as these are always uncommon (and sometimes extremely rare) they have long been of special interest to collectors. Their modern counterpart consists of marks inscribed *Paquebot*, the French term for 'packet boat', adopted by the UPU in 1897. This mark is often found on mail posted on board ship, franked with the stamps of one country and landed in another, and provides a way of cancelling stamps from abroad. *Paquebot* marks are used all over the world, but are nevertheless sufficiently uncommon as to excite considerable interest. Apart from the internationally used French word, other variants and renderings occur, including the Flemish *Paketboot*. There are other marks by which ships' mail can be recognized and these include *Vapore* (Italian for 'steamer'), *Buzón vapor* (Spanish for 'steamer box'), *Schiffsbrief* (German for ship letter), and its Danish equivalent *Skibsbrev*. Mail landed from British warships bore a postmark 'Received from HM Ships', but this was altered to 'Post Office Maritime Mail' during the Second World War to accommodate mail from Allied ships. An unusual kind of maritime marking found mainly in Australia and New Zealand is inscribed 'Loose letter'. Australian postmarks inscribed 'Ship Mail Room', however, have no maritime significance since they merely signify the section of the post office in Melbourne or Sydney that handled the letter prior to onward transmission by sea. Many of the cruise liners have special postal facilities and use attractive pictorial cancellers on tourist mail.

Collectors of cross-Channel mail prize the

Souvenir cover from the maiden voyage of RMS 'Queen Mary', 1936, showing American stamps cancelled by the Southampton Paquebot mark

markings bearing the letters MB (movable box) or BM (*boite mobile*), with the names of seaports. A service introduced in the 1850s permitted the late posting of mail aboard the Channel steamers, which had special iron letterboxes chained to their decks. On arrival at the destination the boxes were unlocked and their contents taken to the nearest post office where the special BM or MB marks were applied. These marks were used at Southampton, London, Le Havre and Saint-Malo and continued until the outbreak of the Second World War. There have also been mail facilities on ferries between Britain and Ireland (Kingstown or Dun Laoghaire to Holyhead) and on the west coast of Scotland, between Greenock and Ardrishaig, and in both cases special postmarks were applied to mail posted on board or handled in transit. The Greenock–Ardrishaig marks were particularly interesting since they bore the names of famous old steamers like the *Columba* and the *Iona*, and their presence on otherwise ordinary Edwardian postcards can boost their value from a few pence to many pounds. There have even been special marks applied to mail salvaged from shipwreck. These are scarce and highly prized on account of the tragic circumstances surrounding them.

Railway mails

Transmission of mail by railway began in 1838 in England and spread to every other country with a railway system. Soon the processing of mail in transit was speeded up by attaching special carriages to trains so that sorters could deal with the mailbags picked up *en route*. Even to this day the travelling post offices (TPOs) attached to inter-city trains offer posting facilities and mail posted in the special boxes at the side of the carriage receives a distinctive postmark which may be recognized by having the names of two or more towns (indicating the route) or the initials TPO, RPO, SC (sorting carriage), ST (sorting tender). Railway mail

right **Souvenir cover from the maiden voyage of the liner 'QE2', 1969**

Railway postmarks of France and Germany; pictorial postmark of the Europa Ferry, Denmark; cancellation of the Oslo–Brevik railway route (45%)

from other parts of the world may be identified by the words *Ambulant* (French), *Ambulancia* (Spanish), often abbreviated to AMB., *Bahnpost* (German), sometimes including the word *Zug* or *Z* (train), *Eisenbahn* or *Eisenb.* (German for railway), or *Banen* (Danish and Norwegian). The words *Bahnhof* (German) and *Ferrovia* (Italian) indicate posting at railway stations and are not of such great interest since they are much more common than items posted on the trains themselves. Similarly British postmarks with RSO (railway suboffice) merely indicated the status of certain post offices at the turn of the century, and in many cases they were nowhere near a railway line but received mailbags which, at some point or other in transmission, had been handled by rail. Many railway postmarks have unusual shapes: oval (Germany and Austria), scalloped (French) or rectangular (the Benelux countries). As in British marks the presence of two or more town names usually denotes a railway mark.

Military mails

This mail, sometimes known as forces' postal history, is an enormous field since special facilities for soldiers' and seamen's letters have existed in many countries since the eighteenth century; such letters were often transmitted at reduced rates or free of postage altogether. For security reasons the locations of Field Post Offices (FPO) and Army Post Offices (APO) are invariably cloaked in anonymity, but the datestamps have serial numbers which assist their identification. In addition to covers and cards from every campaign from the Napoleonic Wars to Vietnam and Northern Ireland, there are censored items,

prisoner of war mail, and even the poignant letters from concentration and displaced persons' camps.

Local postal history

An interesting collection can be formed pertaining to the postal history of your own town, district or county, starting with postmarks and covers salvaged from your own mail. Old postcard albums and bundles of family correspondence will yield many obsolete postmarks and most stamp dealers maintain a stock of material, usually with a strong local flavour, from legal and business accumulations that often go back for centuries. In concentrating on local postal history you should not neglect the meter marks used by business firms, nor even the postage paid impressions now widely used on bulk postings of circulars and mail-order packets. If you are collecting in Britain you should in time be able to trace the development of the posts in your area from the earliest name stamps of the eighteenth century, the mileage marks (showing the distance from London) up to 1828, the undated stamps of the smaller offices up to 1860, and the wide range of datestamps used down to the present day, including machine cancellations, slogans, special handstamps, surcharge and explanatory marks, parcel postmarks and modern covers with phosphor dots indicating electronic sorting. Most European countries yield a similar range of material, dating from the seventeenth century. United States and Canadian postmarks date from the mid-eighteenth century; Australian, New Zealand and South African postmarks from the nineteenth century.

17 Cinderella philately

In the fairy tale Cinderella was the poor girl who was despised and exploited, but ended up as the belle of the ball and the bride of Prince Charming. That is also the story of so many of the byways of philately that were neglected or despised by the majority of collectors but have now attained a fair measure of respectability. The chief stigma attached to them is that they are not listed in the standard stamp catalogues, and as collectors tended to follow those arbiters quite blindly they would not admit these items to their albums. There have always been a few independent spirits who felt that things only became interesting where the catalogues left off and they pioneered interest in the Cinderellas of philately or revived an interest that had existed in the infancy of the hobby but had long lain dormant. Moreover, with the trend towards greater specialization, collectors concentrating on a single country have been more inclined to spread their net to include all the odds and ends which the catalogues seldom have the space to list.

The leading category of Cinderellas comprises all those postage stamps whose only failing is that they were not issued by a government postal administration. At one time these stamps were fully listed but gradually the catalogues weeded them out as pressure on space increased. Even to this day, however, Stanley Gibbons continues to list the Trinidad 'Lady McLeod' and the one and only issue of Tierra del Fuego, though both were non-governmental issues of local validity. Many of the private posts existed because of the inability or unwillingness of government systems to provide an adequate service, such as house to house delivery. In Russia the 'Zemstvo' system was virtually integrated into the imperial network but it was left to each *zemstvo* (district) to issue its own distinctive stamps, of which many hundreds were produced from the 1860s till the 1917 Revolution. Private posts operated in many of the towns and districts of Germany till the early years of this century and can be recognized by such inscriptions as *Privatpost* and *Stadtbrief* (town letter). Stamps inscribed *Bypost* (town post) were issued in many parts of Scandinavia. The local posts in America issued stamps several years before the federal Post Office and continued into the 1850s, and many towns in the Confederate States produced their own stamps during the American Civil War. Distinctive stamps were issued by carriers, such as Wells Fargo and American Express, by steamship companies all over the world and, nearer the present day, by many of the pioneer airlines. In Britain local posts were operated by the colleges of Oxford and Cambridge and, for a brief period in the 1860s, by circular delivery companies who undercut the Post Office. Stamps of a sort – now termed 'local carriage labels' by the British

stamp trade – have been issued in recent years by a number of offshore islands, such as Lundy, Herm, Jethou, Shuna and Pabbay. Where a genuine service exists and the stamps are of low denomination and modest in frequency no harm is done, but all too often the offshore islands have acquired a bad name for prolific issues of excessively high face value, with little or no service to justify their existence. It has even been proved that 'stamps' purporting to come from the island of Soay off Skye were being produced by a London dealer without the knowledge of the owner of the island, far less his permission, and this has now been roundly condemned as a complete fabrication.

Fantasies and forgeries

The collector's term for such material is bogus, though the French prefer the more whimsical *timbre de phantasie* (fantasy stamp). There have been many examples of this in the past and some bogus stamps have even acquired a measure of desirability. The stamps of Counani, Deh Sedang and Clipperton Island were produced by confidence tricksters who used them to induce the gullible to invest their money in colonial projects in these non-existent countries. Civil war provides a marvellous opportunity for entrepreneurs who are quick to provide the rebels with a postal service – complete with stamps which can then be marketed on the other side of the world where their antecedents cannot be questioned. The stamps of the South Moluccas (Maluku Selatan) may have been produced in good faith, but were never issued. More doubtful are the stamps allegedly issued by Eritrea in its fight against Ethiopia, and many of the stamps of Biafra were mysteriously produced in Europe after the Nigerian civil war had ended. Often these issues do not live up to the expectations of their promoters and are then dumped on the philatelic market, ending up as cheap packet material. It is unfortunate that they eventually

Non-governmental stamps with a limited or local validity from Denmark, Scotland, Norway, Lundy, Herm in the Channel Islands, Germany, the United States and Turkey (66%)

Bogus stamps from 'free' Albania, Azerbaijan, the South Moluccas, and Epirus (165%)

come to rest in the albums of children who have spent their pocket money on such rubbish, subsequently discover their true nature and become disillusioned with the hobby as a result.

Far less of a problem today than it was a century ago is forgery. Even relatively common items were forged for sale to collectors who lacked the well-illustrated catalogues we now possess and found such 'album weeds' hard to detect. These early forgeries were comparatively crude and present little or no problem today. Forgeries still exist and are much more subtle and skilful, but as the forgers now concentrate on the very expensive items they are hardly likely to present any problems for the beginner. Nowadays forgers tend to work with genuine stamps but add a fake overprint or postmark to enhance the value of otherwise cheap material. Stamps forged to deceive the postal authorities, however, are often worth more than the genuine article. The best example of this is the so-called Stock Exchange forgery of the British shilling stamp, which is thought to have netted several thousand pounds for its perpetrator. A more modern case concerns the twopenny stamp commemorating the opening of the Sydney Harbour Bridge in 1932. The genuine stamp exists either intaglio, perf. 11 and unwatermarked, or letterpress, perf. 10½ with a multiple watermark. The forgers got things rather muddled by producing quite good imitations by letterpress – but on unwatermarked paper perf. 11. As quite a large number are believed to have got into circulation they could turn up on old letters of the period.

Labels

Advertising labels are not as widely used today as they once were, their role having been overtaken by commemorative stamps. At the turn of the century, however, when commemoratives were few and far between, labels were extensively used, both to publicize events such as exhibitions and conferences, but also to celebrate historic anniversaries. They enjoyed a large following and there were even special catalogues and periodicals devoted to erinnophily (from German *Erinnerung* = 'commemoration' and Greek *philos* = 'love'). It got out of hand when several hundred different labels were published in connection with the 1900 Paris Exposition, and as commemorative stamps became more plentiful collectors turned to them instead. Nevertheless publicity and commemorative labels are still produced and are even enjoying something of a comeback.

Christmas seals were invented by a Danish postal official named Einar Holbøll and were first produced in Denmark in 1904; they spread to the other Scandinavian countries shortly afterwards and were adopted by France, the United States, Canada and other countries during the First World War. To this day Christmas seals continue to enjoy semi-official status in Scandinavia, and also in South Africa where they are produced in booklets sold over the post office counter. In more recent years similar labels have been produced for use on Easter greetings and are now widely used by many charities. Originally intended to raise funds for the campaign against tuberculosis, Christmas seals are used to aid the handicapped and children's charities, a role filled in some countries by the charity stamps already mentioned. Some of the modern Scandinavian seals are printed in sheets with a composite design, each label bearing but a small portion of it, and this encourages collectors to keep the sheets intact.

The most popular group of labels are those produced in connection with exhibitions, especially those pertaining to philately. In Britain they go all the way back to 1890 when remaindered colonial postage stamps were overprinted LPE in honour of the London Philatelic Exhibition. Obsolete stamps were used as souvenirs of other philatelic exhibitions and congresses, with a suitable overprint, and this practice was also widely adopted in Europe. In addition to the labels, designed for the adornment of mail posted at these events, are the pre-publicity labels which have long been a feature of the major national and international exhibitions, and the souvenir sheets. The latter often reproduce obsolete stamps, often produced from the same dies as the originals under licence from the postal administration, but have no franking validity. Some of these sheets are of interest, occasionally taking the form of proofs pulled from the original die, or showing the colour separations used in multicolour stamp production.

Charity seals from Hungary, Yugoslavia, for the Spanish Civil War, from France, Mexico, Thailand, Sweden, the United States, New Zealand and Rhodesia, raising funds for orphans, troop comforts, anti-TB funds and the handicapped (177%)

Tax stamps

There are several categories of stamp which, not being intended for postal use, are ignored by the stamp catalogues though they are just as collectable. Like local stamps and postal stationery, they were more widely collected in the nineteenth century and were often listed by the catalogues, till pressure of space led to their removal. Adhesive stamps to denote the prepayment of taxes have a much older history than adhesive postage stamps. Stamps embossed on white or blue paper and affixed to parchment legal documents by tiny lead staples, secured at the back by stamp-sized labels, date back to the reign of William and Mary in the seventeenth century and it was a Stamp Act governing their use in the American colonies that was one of the major causes of the War of Independence in 1776. When paper replaced parchment it became possible to emboss the tax stamps direct on to the document, a practice which is still in use, but by that time

adhesive stamps were being used for all manner of other taxes – on gloves, wig powder, dice, playing cards, gramophone records, tobacco, wines and spirits, ale, patent medicines, matches at various times in different countries. Adhesive stamps have also been used in the prepayment of entertainment taxes, for the payment of fines and court fees, for passports and consular services such as visas, sales taxes and receipts on all but the smallest transactions. Adhesive stamps may even be found on old cheques, though later embossed stamps were preferred, as in legal documents. Tax stamps are known as fiscals in Britain and revenues in America and enjoy a strong following on both sides of the Atlantic; the American stamps are fully listed and priced in the Scott catalogues. The use of such stamps postally has been sanctioned from time to time and this has already been mentioned. Furthermore, because they have often been printed by the same companies as produced the postage

Revenue or fiscal stamps from Belgium, the United States, Guyana, Egypt, New South Wales, Great Britain, New Zealand, Canada and China (154%)

Labels used by the United States Post Office for resealing opened or damaged packets (150%)

stamps they have a strong affinity with the latter and sometimes use similar designs, distinguished only by the inscriptions.

Stamps for other non-postal purposes

Before the telegraph service was nationalized in 1870 many companies in Britain issued special stamps for use on telegram forms. The Post Office took over these services and issued its own stamps from 1876 till 1882 using the same designs as some of the postage stamps but with different inscriptions. Ordinary stamps were used in 1870–6 and also since 1882. Separate issues, using the basic design of contemporary fiscal stamps with an overprint, were made for military telegraphs at army camps and bases in many parts of the British Empire till 1901. Distinctive telegraph stamps were used in the United States from 1850 till 1946, the last series portraying Samuel Morse, inventor of the code that bears his name. Telegraph stamps, both private and government issues, were extensively used in Austria, Germany, India, Switzerland and many Latin American countries. Spanish stamps punctured by a large hole denote telegraphic usage. Telephone stamps were issued by France, Belgium, Canada, the United States, Denmark and Britain from the 1880s till the First World War to pay fees on telephone calls and television stamps are now used in the payment of licence fees. Savings stamps are another interesting category that is now receiving greater attention. Although National Savings stamps are now a thing of the past in Britain their place has been taken by the special stamps used to save up for the payment of TV licences, telephone bills and fuel charges. Insurance stamps for unemployment, sickness and social-security benefits date from 1909 in Britain and are now widely used in many countries. The British stamps have had scant attention, mainly because the stamped cards have to be surrendered to the authorities and used specimens seldom come into the hands of collectors, but in other countries, where the stamps are retained by the employer if not the employee, they are more accessible. New Zealand employment insurance stamps, with their wealth of overprints, are popular with collectors and are now listed by at least one catalogue.

Registration labels from Mexico, Malta, Finland, Australia, Egypt and Austria, illustrating the diversity of styles and colours

Airmail etiquettes from Fiji, the United States, Australia, Finland, Japan, Sweden, Kenya, New Zealand and Iceland; the bottom row incorporates airline insignia

Stickers and etiquettes

There are also several categories of stickers or labels used by most postal administrations in connection with various services. Mention has already been made of the registration stamps issued by Canada and other countries, but there are also the countless varieties of registration label now in universal use. These were pioneered by the German states in the 1860s, spread to Sweden in 1874 and the United States in 1883, were formally adopted by the UPU in 1906 and introduced to many countries (including Britain) the following year. The UPU laid down the basic design: a large R in the left-hand panel, with the name of the post office and the serial number of the registered letter on the right. Though blue ink was supposed to be used in printing them, registration labels have always varied considerably in colour, layout and inscriptions. As every post office has had its own distinctive labels at some time or another the number of possible varieties for Britain alone runs into many

Explanatory labels used in most countries to denote fragile or perishable packages requiring special handling *top row;* **international parcel post labels** *2nd row;* **small packet and letter packet labels, Canadian 1st Class Mail label** *3rd row;* **explanatory and Certified Mail labels** *4th row;* **labels for use on philatelic mail** *5th row;* **express and special delivery labels** *6th–9th rows*

thousands, while the worldwide total must be truly astronomical.

Etiquette is the term for airmail lables or stickers, from the name used in France where they originated in August 1918. The earliest etiquettes were inscribed *Par Avion* in black on red paper and were used on mail carried on the Paris–Saint-Nazaire service. Etiquettes spread to the United States in 1919 and Britain, Denmark, Holland and Sweden in 1920. Thereafter they rapidly became universal and the UPU laid down guidelines for their design. The majority are printed in blue and show the French expression *Par Avion* with the equivalent in the national language. Many of them incorporate emblems of airlines or motifs symbolizing flight and quite a few examples in recent years have included inscriptions of a commemorative nature. Etiquettes issued by Czechoslovakia (1932) and

certain Portuguese colonies (1932–46) were actually used to denote prepayment of airmail fees and strictly speaking should be classed as stamps, but they are ignored by most stamp catalogues.

There are many other kinds of sticker that the collector may encounter. There are labels for certified mail or recorded delivery, express and special delivery, special handling of collectors' mail, the resealing of damaged packets and a wide range of explanatory labels used in many countries on undelivered mail returned to the sender. Customs labels and censor labels relate to the examination of letters and packets in times of peace and war, the latter being of special interest to forces' postal historians. Even trading stamps, produced under the same security conditions as postage and revenue stamps, are now receiving serious attention from philatelists.

18 Specialized philately

The collector who decides to concentrate on a single country, or even a single period of one country's issues, will inevitably go into the subject much more deeply than the general collector. He will not be content with one example of each stamp, mint and used, but will thoroughly explore every aspect of the stamps. The differences arising from production over a period of years have already been touched on in the section dealing with the anatomy of stamps (p. 42). The specialist must become adept at using a quartz lamp, not only to identify fluorescent or phosphorescent treatment of stamps, but to recognize phosphor bands applied by letterpress from those applied by photogravure, and not only differing widths of phosphor but various colours of phosphor – often discernible only by measurement in angstrom units.

The collector who specializes in New Zealand stamps will quickly become engrossed in the 'Adsons' – the nickname for the 1893 definitives which had advertisements for all manner of branded goods and patent medicines printed on the backs. The layout of these advertisements was changed on two subsequent occasions, so it is possible to reconstruct entire sheets of these stamps showing first, second and third settings. As all values from ½d to 1s were treated in this manner and different colours of ink were used, the study of the Adsons is a lifetime hobby in itself. Fortunately this experiment was short-lived, but to collect the later issues it is necessary to be able to distinguish the experimental papers

used in the inter-war period, known as De La Rue, Jones, Art, Cowan and Wiggins Teape paper respectively. The wartime stamps are known on first fine paper, second fine paper and coarse paper, further subdivided according to whether the mesh of the paper is horizontal or vertical. Modern British stamps are incredibly complicated and can be classified according to the paper (white or cream), the gum (arabic, polyvinyl alcohol or Dextrin tinted), the surface (glossy or chalky), the watermark (Tudor crown, St Edward's crown, multiple crown or none at all), with graphite lines on the reverse, a combination of graphite lines and phosphor bands, or phosphor bands alone, in various positions.

Flaws – constant and occasional

Apart from all the factors in stamp production which may make for subtle differences there are the errors and flaws that distinguish philately as one of the few collectables in which something less than perfect may actually be worth more than the perfect article. Each printing process is liable to produce its own brand of imperfection. Intaglio stamps may be found with signs of plate wear, or with weak or double entries – portions printing faultily because the plate was not properly treated by the transfer roller – and the correction of these flaws may result in re-entries or areas re-engraved on the plate by hand and therefore slightly different from the original. Similar flaws may occur through faulty etching

Errors on stamps.
Top: inverted overprint (Greece), inverted surcharge (North Borneo), inverted centre (Panama); *bottom:* strip of three stamps from Burundi, two with the correct overprint 'Royaume du Burundi' and the centre stamp with the error 'Royaume du Royaume' (152%)

of the cylinder in photogravure production, and these flaws can subsequently be eradicated by retouching. Thus stamps showing flaws and retouches provide a 'before and after' effect. In lithography the commonest failing arises from the transfers getting slightly creased while they are laid down on the stones, and this can result in some startling effects, the best known being the NFW flaw on the 1911 1-cent stamps of Newfoundland. Letterpress stamps are a fertile field since their plates are prone to damage and any crack, scratch or dent in the plate may result in a corresponding white flaw on the stamps.

Where flaws, re-entries and retouches are constant they usually attain listing in the more advanced catalogues. Other flaws are more ephemeral. Confetti flaws, appearing as white circles on the face of the stamp, are caused by tiny circles of paper (punched out by the perforator) adhering to the printing plate and thus preventing ink from getting to the paper at that point. In photogravure a device known as a doctor blade keeps the ink spread evenly, but a slight jump in the blade can result in a coloured or colourless line appearing over several stamps. Such doctor-blade flaws are often quite spectacular, but are of little more than curiosity value. The same applies to colour shifts, due to faulty registration of the printing cylinders or plates, but likewise they are of interest to the specialist. They are ignored by the catalogues, but missing colours, or the inversion of one or more colour in relation to the rest, are noteworthy.

Plating

Minor but constant flaws, frame breaks, weak entries and re-entries serve a useful purpose, enabling the really dedicated philatelist to reconstruct an entire sheet of stamps. Known as 'plating', this became popular with the earliest collectors since British stamps bore corner letters from AA to TL which encouraged them to try and reconstruct the sheet layout. Actually, it was greatly complicated by the fact that many plates were used in the long life of the Penny Red, and even the Penny Black used eleven plates in the space of less than a year. Each of these plates had minute characteristics, such as peculiarities in the letters and stars in the corners, so that

specialists soon learn to assign stamps to the exact plate. From 1858 to 1880 British stamps not only had corner letters but tiny plate numbers, so plate reconstruction became simply a matter of getting hold of large enough quantities of stamps.

Sheet margins

Plating is quite impossible when it comes to most of the modern stamps, but the specialist finds plenty of scope in studying the sheet margins. From 1881 to 1947 British stamps had control numbers and letters in one corner for accounting purposes and specialists therefore collect control blocks and strips. They were superseded by cylinder numbers which identify the printing cylinder used in photogravure. As sheets are printed two at a time, side by side, they may be distinguished by the presence of a full stop after the number, and thus specialists have to collect 'dot' and 'no-dot' numbers. Multicolour stamps also have colour dabs, known as 'traffic lights', and these are also collected in corner blocks.

Ancillary material

The really dedicated specialist will not be content merely with the stamps themselves but will search for ancillary material. This might consist of Post Office notices announcing new postal charges or a change in rates; announcements publicizing design competitions; artists' preliminary sketches and finished artwork; proofs taken from the master die at various stages of the engraving; proofs from the printing plate, in black ink or the issued colour; colour trials (testing the effect of various colour combinations); essays (designs which may have been taken all the way to actual printing but which never went into full production); progressive proofs, showing each of the colour separations in multicolour printing; imperforate proofs and printers' samples; and stamps overprinted 'Specimen' or its equivalent in other languages, such as *Müster* (German), *Muestra* (Spanish), for distribution to the UPU or to philatelic journalists as publicity material. The issued stamps might be represented in the collection by plate or cylinder blocks, gutter pairs, traffic light blocks or even entire sheets if they were small enough. There would be a range of shades to show the different printings, not to mention the changes in paper, gum, watermark and phosphor bands during the lifetime of the issue, and a corresponding array of the used stamps, possibly also including covers with unusual combinations of denominations to make up various postal rates, special postmarks and incorrect or irregular usage. Finally the collection would not be complete without the presentation packs, first-day covers, PHQ cards and other official souvenirs that attend each new issue. Thus a set of stamps that might occupy a single page or less in a general collection can be expanded by the specialist to fill a whole album.

Despite the use of the word 'stamp' in their inscriptions, these labels had no postal validity (150%)

19 Arranging and writing up a collection

Unless you stick exclusively to the various printed albums mentioned earlier you will soon be faced with the problem of arranging your stamps and writing up the album pages. Of course it is entirely up to the individual to please himself how he classifies his stamps and annotates their pages, but over the years excellent and highly satisfactory methods have been evolved, and these may be studied by viewing the sheets on display at any stamp exhibition. A number of techniques have been hotly debated and there are many collectors who dislike the use of typewriting or mounting strips such as the Hawid range, while others maintain that typewriting is a reasonable alternative for those unable or unwilling to master the art of calligraphy, and that so long as the current pre-occupation with unmounted mint stamps prevails there is no alternative to using Hawid strips. But whichever system you adopt there are some useful hints to consider before you actually stick your stamps on the page.

Laying out the album page

First of all it is advisable to lay your stamps out on the blank page and try to make a balanced arrangement that gives maximum eye appeal. It is better to have too few than too many stamps on each page. An ideal number for the average album page would be about 20 small-format definitives and 12 to 15 large stamps, or even fewer if they are really big, as so many recent stamps are. Thus it should be possible to accommodate most definitive sets quite comfortably on a single page, but it is always better to split the set into two if one page would become overcrowded. If you have a set of 16 stamps, all of the same size and format, it is tempting to take the easy road and lay them out in four rows of 4. This may be symmetrical but it is monotonous. It would be better to adopt a pyramid principle starting with the lowest denomination on its own, then a row of two, followed by a row of three, two rows of four and finally the two highest denominations on their own at the foot of the page. Such a system has the advantage of flexibility since additional denominations – new values or changes of colour – can be inserted without too much upheaval and often no more than the rearrangement of a single row. Another variant of the pyramid would be rows with a constant left-hand margin and rows of one, two, three, four or more stamps so that the right-hand margin slopes. Again, new stamps can be added without much inconvenience. A diamond layout, with rows of one, two, three, four, three, two and one stamps, also permits additions, working from the centre row of the diamond.

Much more ingenuity may be required, however, to lay out a series of mixed shapes and sizes.

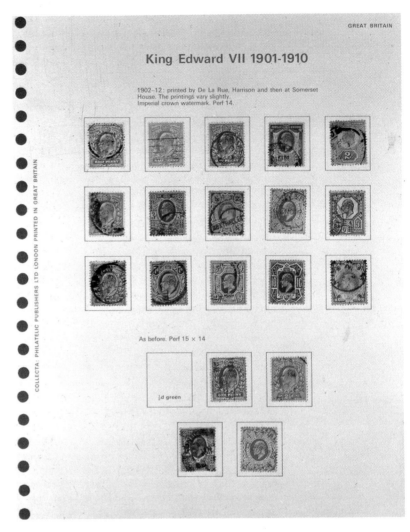

COLLECTA PHILATELIC PUBLISHERS LTD LONDON PRINTED IN GREAT BRITAIN

GREAT BRITAIN

King Edward VII 1901-1910

1902–12: printed by De La Rue, Harrison and then at Somerset House. The printings vary slightly. Imperial crown watermark. Perf 14.

As before. Perf 15 × 14

½d green

Typical page from one of the modern printed one-country albums, allowing a space for each stamp, with appropriate captions

In this case it is permissible to break the sequence of face value, to group the vertical designs in one row and the horizontal stamps in another. However you lay out these stamps you should always try to achieve balance, and it is better to put individual stamps in a row of their own if they cannot be matched with another.

Annotating the collection

Do not start mounting the stamps too near the top of the page; this is a common failing among beginners. Leave two or three centimetres depth as a minimum, so that the heading and details of the issue can be inserted. How much space you require will depend on the amount of annotation you feel is necessary. Opinions vary as to how much annotation is ideal. It would not be sufficient to head a page of current British stamps 'Decimal Series, 1971'. Fuller details might state, '15 February 1971. Decimal Currency. Design from a plaster cast by Arnold Machin, R.A., Photogravure by Harrison & Sons, High Wycombe. Chalky cream paper. Two phosphor bands, Perf. 15 × 14.' This could then be followed by a superficially similar series headed: '1972. As above, but printed on fluorescent white paper.' When it comes to commemoratives and other special issues it is best to devote a separate page to each set, with mint stamps at the top and used stamps mounted below. Avoid mixing mint and used stamps where possible and remember that it is always better to leave a blank space, in case you eventually get the stamp you are missing, than to mount the stamps one after the other and then have to do the entire page again when the wanted stamp turns up. The headings for commemoratives would include the date and the technical details as for the definitives, but could be further elaborated by brief notes about the motifs, or the reason for the issue. A certain amount of ancillary material might be included, such as photographs of the subjects on which the stamp designs were based, but this should always be kept to a minimum so as not to detract from the stamps themselves.

The actual method of annotation varies from person to person, depending on their skill and the neatness of their handwriting. Some collectors of the older school prefer a copperplate style of writing, but the italic script now taught in many British schools is neater and more legible. Most collectors prefer some kind of printing, using upper- and lower-case lettering rather than block capitals. A draughtsman's pen or mapping pen and black india ink are the best materials for calligraphy, but an ordinary fountain pen is better than ballpoint (which is liable to smudge and may affect the stamps), and pencil should be avoided unless the layout is in a transitional stage. There are various forms of stencil that enable you to produce very even lettering, and the sets of transfers like Letraset result in a highly professional job, though they are relatively expensive and very time-consuming. Capitals and underlining can be done in red

or some other contrasting colour, but do not overdo this or the over-all effect will be marred. Some collectors get really carried away and produce pages resembling the illuminated manuscripts of the medieval monks, with the result that the stamps are totally lost in a welter of Gothic curlicues.

Typewriting is now much more acceptable, though judges still tend to mark down competitive entries rather unfairly if presented in this form. Using a typewriter is more complicated than ordinary handwriting since you need to work out very carefully the position of each stamp, with pencil dots on the squares of the page, before placing the sheet in the machine. Because of the stiff cartridge paper used, and the further complication of linen hinges and glassine interleaving, it is difficult to get album pages properly aligned in the typewriter and then keep them that way before you get to the foot of the page, but with practice you should be able to master the technique. The modern electric typewriters with a plastic carbon ribbon can give a beautiful effect. If using an ordinary typewriter ribbon do make sure that it is reasonably fresh, and that the typewriter keys are kept clean, since there is nothing more unsightly than clogged lettering.

In annotating a specialized collection it may be desirable to include sketches to illustrate, greatly enlarged, the flaws and retouches which appear on the stamps. Tiny arrows with an adhesive backing can be purchased from stamp dealers and are useful for pin-pointing special features on stamps, but be careful to avoid sticking them over the stamps themselves. Line drawings should be kept as simple as possible and if you lack the necessary draughtsman's skill the same result may be achieved by using enlarged photographs.

Presenting ancillary material

In a postal-history collection items such as, covers, entire letters and cards can be mounted with stamp hinges, but transparent photographic mounting corners are much better, and these should also be used when mounting FDCs, presentation packs and booklets.

Where a cover has interesting postmarks on the back it is quite a good idea to mount a photocopy of the reverse on the same page, below the cover itself, and attention can be drawn to the various postal markings in the writing-up.

The greatest leeway in annotation is allowed in thematics and it is here that the creative talents of the collector come to the fore. This may range from extensive background notes on the subjects including press cuttings and photographs, though you should not go to the extreme (which one occasionally sees in stamp exhibitions) of a page with a single stamp and masses and masses of writing. Remember that you are making a stamp collection based around stamps, not writing a book!

Page from a collection devoted to the theme of coins on stamps, with annotation by electric typewriter. The stamps are held in position by Hawid transparent strips with black backing

20 The beginning of philately

Dr John Gray of the British Museum was one of the men who contested Rowland Hill's title as inventor of the adhesive postage stamp. He took a close interest in postal reform and on the day the Penny Black and Twopence Blue were issued he purchased examples of them to keep as a memento of the occasion. He could therefore claim, with some justification, to have been the world's first stamp collector. Later he went on to compile one of the early British stamp catalogues and also published sets of gummed titles which could be cut up and stuck as headings in the stamp album. Apart from Dr Gray there must have been other men and women who perceived the innate interest in these tiny scraps of paper and began forming collections of them. By the 1850s, when stamps had spread to a score and more countries, and the number of stamps on a simplified basis had already run into hundreds, stamp collecting was well established. References to this strange new mania began to be made in newspapers and periodicals, and, more significantly, advertisements of stamps wanted or for sale also appeared by that time. Edward Stanley Gibbons was born in the same year as the Penny Black and began dealing in stamps in 1856, in Plymouth, and other dealers were also trading in stamps by that time. Stanley Gibbons Ltd celebrated its centenary in 1956 and nine years later held an exhibition at the Festival Hall, London to mark the centenary of the company's first catalogue.

Oscar Berger-Levrault and Alfred Potiquet both began publishing catalogues in France in 1861 and soon there were regular magazines devoted to the hobby. One of the earliest was the *Stamp Collectors Magazine* which made its debut in February 1863, and contained in its opening pages a very vivid account of the open-air selling and swapping of stamps conducted in Birchin Lane, Cheapside, in London, and the similar *al fresco* meetings of timbromaniacs in the gardens of the Luxembourg and the Tuileries in Paris. Timbromania, the original pseudo-scientific name for stamp collecting (from the French word *timbre*, 'stamp') was soon replaced by something more dignified, if less easy to pronounce. Again it was a Frenchman, Georges Herpin, who coined the word philately, but his logic was as faulty as his grasp of Greek (*philos* = 'love', *a* = 'not', *telos* = 'tax'). He tried to convey the idea of something on which no tax or charge was due because it has been prepaid, and thus ended up with a word literally meaning a lover of no taxes. Some have argued that atelophily would have been more correct. Significantly the Greeks use the term *philoteleia* and omit the negative element, implying that we are lovers of taxes rather than of the stamps that signify their payment.

Among the pioneer collectors was the Rev. F. J. Stainforth who organized the first indoor meetings after the police had begun to discourage obstruction in Birchin Lane. In the 1860s collectors used to meet on Saturday afternoons at the Rectory, All Hallows, Staining – the Dickensian ring of the name is hardly surprising, since it actually features in the novel *Dombey and Son*. Here the good rector held court over his cronies, who included Charles Viner, editor of the *Stamp Collectors Magazine*; Mount Brown, publisher of one of the earliest catalogues; Judge Philbrick; and Sir Daniel Cooper, who became President of the Philatelic Society, London, when it was founded in 1869. A society had been formed in Paris some four years earlier but it did not last long. The London Society, now the Royal Philatelic Society, is still in existence and if not the biggest is certainly the most prestigious in the world. Several women featured prominently in the early history of the hobby, including Charlotte Tebay who helped organize the earliest London exhibition, and Adelaide Lucy Fenton who was a prolific writer in the stamp magazines – but like certain lady novelists of an earlier generation, she preferred to write under the masculine pen name of Herbert Camoens.

The growth of clubs and exhibitions

The English School was noted for its general approach to philately, whereas the French School had a more scientific bent. They paid greater attention to the minute variations in their stamps and, as we have seen, it was one of them, Dr J. A. Legrand, who invented the perforation gauge (1866) and wrote the earliest treatise on watermarks a year later. The Europeans followed the French, whereas the Americans followed the English style, but by the 1870s the two had merged and philately had developed into the exact science we know today. It went through a period of stagnation in the 1870s (the *Stamp Collectors Magazine* was forced into oblivion in 1874 for lack of support), but it managed to weather the doldrums and by the 1880s had gained such an international influence that it was possible to stage the first exhibitions open to collectors from many countries. In Britain such cities as Glasgow, Liverpool and Bath were flourishing centres of stamp dealing, but gradually the bigger dealers gravitated towards the metropolis and to this day London is the centre of the stamp world. Very few clubs were organized outside London, Manchester being the first provincial city to boast its own philatelic society, but this trend developed in the early 1900s. Another major landmark was the holding of the first London exhibition in 1890 and this has become a regular ten-yearly affair since 1950. In 1909 Manchester was the venue for the first

A scene from the London 1980 International Philatelic Exhibition, Earl's Court

Philatelic Congress of Great Britain, an event that is held annually to the present day in various parts of the country, and has produced enough material, in the way of souvenir covers, labels, sheets and postmarks, to make a sizeable collection in itself.

Stamp clubs at local level and congresses and federations at national level developed in Europe, America and in Australasia, and major international exhibitions are now held several times a year. The governing body is the Fédération Internationale de Philatélie, which sets out the rules for competitions and judging and attempts to apply the brake on excessive and unnecessary stamp issues, a growing problem whose solution has so far defeated efforts by the UPU. Most towns of any size now boast at least one stamp club, meeting monthly or even more frequently, where collectors can exchange unwanted duplicates, buy and sell stamps, and attend lectures by prominent philatelists. Information about the clubs in your neighbourhood can usually be obtained from the local public library. There is also a growing tendency for collectors of similar interests and specialization to band together in societies of national or international standing. Though these societies also hold regular meetings the main medium for intercourse is the club magazine in which the latest research is published. Most clubs, at both local and national level, also maintain a club

exchange packet – a system that enables all members to add to their collections with the minimum of expense. Participants mount their unwanted and surplus material in special booklets, adding the price, and send them to the club secretary who makes up a packet that then goes on rotation to the other members, who remove the stamps they want and send their remittances to the secretary. The secretary settles up with the contributors, deducting his operating expenses and a percentage that goes to the club funds.

Museum collections

The monuments to acumen, expertise and sheer dedication to the hobby are those collections now preserved in museums. London is particularly fortunate in having both the collections in the British Library and the National Postal Museum itself. The latter was the brainchild of the late Reginald M. Phillips, whose magnificent collection of British stamps formed the nucleus. The Smithsonian Institution in Washington has one of the world's largest philatelic collections, but excellent displays are to be found in most countries, from Oslo and Ottawa to Christchurch, New Zealand, based on the specimens distributed by the UPU but often including magnificent donations by public-spirited individuals who feel impelled to share their love of stamps with their fellow collectors in perpetuity.

21 Stamp dealing and exhibiting

Young Stanley Gibbons started dealing in stamps in a very modest way, from his father's pharmacy in Plymouth. This was presumably a sideline that gradually got more and more time-consuming, but also more lucrative, so that he was tempted to branch out on his own. The same story could be repeated a thousand times over, for it is how most dealers past and present have got started in the business. Such are the complexities of philately that only someone who has grown up with the hobby from early childhood and has stamps in his blood can really hope to master it. Because stamps are small and easily sent through the post, much of the world's stamp trade is conducted by small dealers, many of them part-timers, operating from their own homes and keeping business overheads to a minimum. It is an intensely competitive business where profit margins are pared to the bone and everyone relies on rapid turnover of stock to keep one jump ahead of his rivals.

For every dealer with an actual retail shop there are perhaps a score whose business is postal or by appointment only. Some of the world's largest dealers operate in quite a modest manner, acting on behalf of a few very wealthy clients who will regularly spend thousands of pounds with them. They are truly international, traversing the world in search of major rarities, attending auctions in London, New York and Sydney, and dealing only in the more expensive items. Their 'office' is their briefcase and a telephone in a hotel suite. At the other end of the scale, however, are the vast majority of dealers, content to make a modest living from sending out approval books (just like the club packets), or publishing lists of specialist material, which they circulate to their clients every few weeks. It would be idle to speculate how much of the world stamp trade relies wholly on the postal system, but at least half of it must be conducted in this way. From the collector's viewpoint it is one of the few hobbies that can be pursued without leaving his armchair, and for this reason it appeals to the housebound and the handicapped, many of whom have also become dealers in due course.

Finding the right dealer

Apart from the excellent directories of dealers, published by such bodies as the Philatelic Traders' Society in Britain and the American Stamp Dealers' Association, the easiest way of contacting a dealer specializing in your field is to scour the classified advertisements in the philatelic magazines. If yours is a popular subject the choice of dealers will be bewildering, but whatever your interests, no matter how esoteric, somewhere there will be at least one dealer specializing in them. As a rule the dealers with a retail shop tend to hold general stocks since they

have to cater to all tastes, whereas the postal dealers are more likely to concentrate on specific subjects. Many of them are leading authorities in their chosen speciality and you can usually rely on their judgment and integrity.

The major cities in which the stamp trade flourishes usually have several shops grouped together. In London, for example, many of the leading dealers are located in and around the Strand where Stanley Gibbons has its premises. Nassau Street in New York and the Rue Drouot in Paris are important venues of the stamp trade. In addition to single shops you will find several dealers under the same roof. In London there is the Strand Stamp Centre and, a few doors farther along, Strand Stamps, both accommodating a number of dealers offering a very wide range of material. Another modern phenomenon is the stamp fair. Many of them are held each month in a fixed venue; others go on circuit through the provincial towns and literally bring the stamp trade to collectors who may not have an opportunity to visit London and the other great centres of the stamp world. This form of trading is now well established in North America, Britain and western Europe, and provides a medium for both dealers with retail shops and those who normally deal by post only. It is a two-way business, since the object is not only to sell to collectors but to buy fresh material from the public. The circuit fairs tend to be more in the nature of buying trips and undoubtedly this technique has yielded some spectacular results: many of the great 'finds' of recent years have come to light in this unusual manner.

Stamp auctions

Purchases by mail order or direct from a stamp shop satisfy the majority of collectors, but there is a third method – the stamp auction. Unlike auctions in the realms of fine art and antiques, which are largely dominated by the dealers, stamp sales are attended by many private collectors, and the farther the auction is from the major trading centres the higher the proportion of collectors. Stamps are often included in general sales operated by provincial auctioneers large and small, and the knowledgeable collector may sometimes get a bargain there since, by and large, these sales do not attract the attention of the philatelic fraternity. On the other hand, stamp auctioneering is a highly skilled business and it has to be admitted that an auctioneer whose main business is fatstock sales is unlikely to know enough about the subtleties and intricacies of philately to do justice to the lotting and describing of such material. No serious collector would entrust his valuable collection to such an uncertain method of disposal but would go to one of the specialist auctioneers. Therefore

Six rare stamps. The values given are approximate: they vary considerably according to the condition of the stamp. *Top:* **Canada, 1851 12d Black Imperforate printed on laid paper, £35,000; Canada, 1897 $5 Olive-green Jubilee issue, £1,500; Mauritius, 1847 'Post Office' 2d Indigo-Blue, £25,000;** *bottom:* **Switzerland (Basel), 1945 Coat of Arms 2½r Carmine, Black and Blue 'The Basel Dove', £4,000; Great Britain, 1891 Queen Victoria £1 Green Jubilee issue, £4,000; United States, 1920 $2 Franklin Orange-red and Black, £650** (157%)

these salerooms do not handle the better material, but now and again a stamp collection, long forgotten, comes to light in a sale of house contents, and then the lucky philatelist who happens to be in the right place at the right moment may hit the jackpot.

The first stamp auction ever recorded took place in Paris in 1865 and five years later J. Walter Scott (who is to American philately what Stanley Gibbons is to British) organized his first sale. Scott introduced the idea to England, organizing an auction in March 1872 which was held at Sotheby's and fetched the then record sum of £253. Although Sotheby's subsequently held a number of stamp auctions, this famous company gradually gave up this side of its business in face of competition from the independent and specialist stamp auctioneers who arose in the 1880s. By the end of the century at least six firms were conducting regular stamp sales. One of these firms – Plumridge & Co. – is still in existence, though it was long ago eclipsed by the giants of the industry, Stanley Gibbons, Harmer's and Robson Lowe (all with headquarters in London and subsidiaries in many parts of the world), and the major provincial companies, such as Warwick & Warwick whose headquarters, the National Philatelic Centre in Warwick, is now an important tourist attraction in the English Midlands.

The stamp auction is where the best of the material comes up for sale and the annual turnover of the more important firms runs to many millions of pounds. In recent years the firm of

Sotheby Parke Bernet has re-entered this lucrative field, and now conducts regular sales in London and New York. At an American auction in April 1980 the famous One Cent Black on Magenta of British Guiana was knocked down for £435,000. This was not only a world record for a single stamp but it justified the claim for this scrap of paper to be the most valuable thing in the world in proportion to its size and weight. Since it first appeared in the saleroom in 1923 this stamp has been a legend. In the Ferrary sale at the Hôtel Drouot, Paris, it fetched the equivalent of £7343 (Ferrary bought it in 1878 for £150). At Harmer's in 1935, however, it failed to reach its reserve of £7,500 but was later sold in America for a sum in the region of £10,000. When Frederick Small sold it in 1970 it made the staggering sum of £100,000 and ten years later it fetched four times that amount, proving conclusively that stamp investment is one way of beating inflation.

Though most auctions are conducted live, it is normal practice for those unable to attend to bid by post, and special bid forms are sent out with the catalogues in advance of each sale. Stamp auction catalogues invariably include an estimated value after each lot description, though if you are really keen to acquire a particular lot you may submit a bid considerably in excess of the estimate. If the bidding stops below your bid you will get the lot for the next stage in the bidding above the last room bid.

As a rule the auctioneer charges commission to the vendor, but in recent years the pernicious

system known as the buyer's premium has begun to creep in as well and this takes the form of a percentage over and above the bid price. Furthermore Value Added Tax in Britain and various forms of sales tax elsewhere have to be taken into consideration. In Britain bids may be VAT inclusive or exclusive: it is therefore important to read the Conditions of Sale printed in the catalogue to know just how much you will be expected to pay before you can collect your purchases.

Buying at auctions is still the best method for the serious collector to acquire rare material, generally at prices below that at which a dealer would offer it, because his profit margin and operating expenses would have to be added. Conversely sale of your collection by auction provides the fairest method, since you will almost certainly get more for your material by letting dealers and other collectors compete with each other, than if you sold outright to a dealer whose differential between buying and selling prices may be quite substantial.

Philatelic bureaux
The one-country collector, particularly the advanced specialist, may choose yet another

method of buying his material. At one time postal administrations regarded philatelists as something of a nuisance and would only negotiate transactions with approved dealers – a system that is adhered to by the Crown Agents who act on behalf of some forty countries, mainly in the Commonwealth. Most countries, however, now operate a philatelic bureau and are fully conscious of the revenue to be derived from direct sales to collectors and dealers alike. Postal administrations with a philatelic bureau advertise regularly in the stamp magazines, and by merely filling up the requisite coupon you may be assured of a regular flow of circulars informing you of all forthcoming issues. With these circulars comes an order form or stock sheet and it is a fairly simple matter nowadays to remit the necessary money, instructions as to the method of payment preferred by the bureau being included on the form. Most bureaux go to enormous trouble to accommodate their clients and their caprices, and whereas a direct approach to a post office counter for cylinder blocks and

gutter pairs may be refused, bureaux are usually only too happy to oblige. Moreover, it is through the bureaux that the material not normally handled by stamp dealers – such as booklets and postal stationery – can easily be purchased.

Although the great bulk of their business is transacted postally, many bureaux also have sales counters located in the largest post offices and sometimes in the postal museums which they also administer in many countries. The more enterprising bureaux also take stands at the leading national and international exhibitions, and as well as having the full range of current stamps and postal stationery on sale they often provide souvenirs of the exhibition in the form of special printings of stamp reproductions on cards, pictorial cachets and even postmarks applied to commemorative covers. The most prestigious of the international exhibitions are honoured by stamps from many parts of the world, and first-day ceremonies are sometimes organized simultaneously in the country itself and also at the exhibition on the opening day.

left **Interior view of the National Philatelic Centre, showing part of the monthly exhibition of rare stamps and postal-history material**

above **The National Philatelic Centre, Warwick**

The courtyard of the National Philatelic Centre, showing the Victorian pillar box. All mail posted in this box receives a special pictorial cancellation, changed each month

Exhibitions today

Stamp exhibitions have been in existence for almost a century and during that time they have changed from being purely confined to competitive and invited displays of stamps by private individuals to become the great crossroads of philately, where dealers and philatelic bureaux congregate and collectors flock from all over the world to examine their merchandise. Purists may decry this trend and feel that the stamp displays have been relegated to a secondary role. The British Philatelic Exhibition was, in fact, first established as a rival to Stampex (the other major national show) to try to get back to a situation where stamp displays were the main attraction, but the organizers were forced to admit the dealers' stands at subsequent shows when the attendance figures turned out to be so disappointing. In Britain Stampex is held in February or March and the BPE in October or November, but there are also numerous regional exhibitions and conventions, usually organized by federations of philatelic societies, and these

shows tend to lay more emphasis on the competitive displays, though dealers' stands are also a major attraction.

A similar pattern is to be found in other countries. The United States probably has the largest number of exhibitions, dealers' and collectors' conventions and national bourses, but exhibitions at club, regional and national level are also staged each year in Europe, Australasia and an increasing number of countries in the Third World. May 6th is Day of the Stamp, an event that allows some countries the opportunity to issue Stamp Day stamps with a charity premium to subsidize clubs and exhibitions. New Zealand organized a National Stamp Week in 1970, an idea that subsequently spread to Australia and has been tried in Britain also. These events are supported by exhibitions.

Those who aspire to take part in the competitive sections of the international exhibitions must first earn a silver medal or a higher award at national level, and this ensures that the standards of the entries in the main annual exhibitions are kept high. To attain this level may take many years of competing in the local club show, gradually improving the layout and writing-up, and acquiring those gems that make all the difference between the mediocre and the first-rate, until the collection is ready for Stampex or BPE. The coveted silver award at national exhibitions, however, is no more than the key to the door and such an entry at international exhibitions may receive only a certificate of participation at the first attempt. Such is the competitive instinct in many stamp collectors that this disappointment will merely spur them on to greater efforts, and over the years they will climb the ladder of international awards, from bronze and bronze-silver medals, through silver, silver-gilt or vermeil awards to small and large gold medals. At the pinnacle of the awards system are the national and international Grand Prix and the special trophies. Thereafter the Grand Prix winners may be invited to exhibit *hors concours* (out of contest) in the Court of Honour, along with the exhibits from the world's most prestigious collections, such as those belonging to Queen Elizabeth II or Prince Rainier of Monaco. It is when you see these dazzling arrays of the great rarities that you appreciate the old adage about stamp collecting being 'the King of Hobbies and Hobby of Kings'. Among the famous collectors of the past were King George V, King Carol of Romania, King Farouk of Egypt and Franklin D. Roosevelt, President of the United States. Today's biggest collectors are more likely to be property tycoons, industrial millionaires, film stars and pop idols, while the greatest rarities are probably owned by investment syndicates and union pension funds. But it is still the hobby of schoolboys and housewives and countless millions of ordinary people all over the world, and it is with them that its enduring strength lies.

22 Reading about stamps

Stamp collectors are extremely fortunate in the vast range of literature at their disposal, from catalogues, handbooks and monographs to commercially published magazines, society journals and the bulletins of the various philatelic bureaux.

All of these have an important role in keeping the collector informed of the latest developments, but stamp catalogues are the indispensable tool of the hobby, without which it would be impossible to put stamps into proper order, far less have any idea of their worth. These philatelic bibles have come a long way from the first faltering lists produced by Potiquet and Berger-Levrault, Dr Gray and Mount Brown in the 1860s. In the same decade Edward Stanley Gibbons in England and J. Walter Scott in America published their first price lists which, over the intervening century, have developed into the Scott and Gibbons catalogues now used all over the English-speaking world. Catalogues

of global coverage are also published in France by Yvert & Tellier and by Zumstein, and in Germany by Michel. General catalogues, such as the Gibbons *Stamps of the World*, generally ignore variations in perforation (other than perforated and imperforate versions), watermark, shade and printing process, but are perfectly adequate for the general and thematic collectors.

At a more advanced level Gibbons publishes the famous 'red' book, dealing with the stamps of the Commonwealth in some detail, major varieties of perforation, watermark, phosphor bands and shade being listed and priced. Gibbons used to publish 2 volumes – green (Europe and colonies) and blue (the rest of the world), but these had to be subdivided into 3 or 4 volumes for each group, and this system has now been further divided into 21 volumes – such has been the growth of new issues in recent years. Separate volumes now deal with all the stamps of the French group of countries, the various

A selection of stamp catalogues, ranging from the simplified 'Stamps of the World' to the highly specialized 'Great Britain: Queen Elizabeth Decimal Issues' *top left*

German postal administrations, China, the Scandinavian group, the Benelux countries and so on. From the collector's viewpoint this system has the advantage that he no longer has to buy more literature than he needs for his own particular interest, and from the publisher's viewpoint it makes the colossal task of listing and pricing all the world's stamps more manageable.

Apart from the general whole-world catalogues, other publishers have concentrated on one-country catalogues, and as well as Scott, Yvert, Zumstein and Michel there are many others in this field, such as Facit (Scandinavia), Bolaffi (Italy) and Prinet (Belgium).

Specialist catalogues
At an even more advanced level there are the specialist catalogues. Again, Stanley Gibbons is pre-eminent in this field with the magnificent *Great Britain Specialised Stamp Catalogue* which now runs to four volumes, dealing respectively with Queen Victorian stamps, the reigns of the four kings (Edward VII–George VI), Elizabethan sterling stamps 1952–71 and Elizabethan decimal currency stamps from 1971 to date. Each volume contains several hundred pages of closely packed information on every conceivable aspect of British philately. Not only are booklets, FDCs and stationery fully listed and priced, but also more out-of-the-way material, such as essays, proofs, colour trials, specimen overprints and telegraph stamps. Though primarily a dealer's price list, catalogues of this type go far beyond this in their encyclopedic coverage and now rank among the major works of reference. Not quite in the same league, but of superlative quality nonetheless, are the specialized catalogues published by Scott (United States), Holmes (Canada), Campbell Paterson (New Zealand) and Robson Lowe (British Commonwealth up to 1952). At the other end of the scale Gibbons also produces low-priced paperbacks in full colour, dealing with the stamps of Britain, the Channel Islands and the Isle of Man, and has recently launched a specialist catalogue of the Channel Islands which is every bit as thorough as the *Great Britain Specialised Stamp Catalogue*.

For collectors of airmails there is Sanabria's *Air Post Catalogue* and the Francis Field range of handbooks, published in America and Britain respectively. There are even priced catalogues devoted to the more popular themes, such as the Olympics, space, religion, paintings, fauna and flora, Europa and sport. Higgins & Gage of America publishes a specialized catalogue of world postal stationery, while David Field of London produces a catalogue devoted to miniature sheets. Priced catalogues dealing with aspects of postal history have also been attempted, but such is the complexity of the subject that these volumes can seldom give a precise value for individual postmarks and usually prefer to compromise by giving a rarity code from A (very common) to F (only two–three examples recorded). There are catalogues of telegraph stamps, railway-letter stamps, local carriage labels, local stamps, airmail etiquettes, stamp booklets and parcel stamps. There is hardly an aspect of philately that has not been covered by a catalogue at some time or another.

Books on philately
When it comes to handbooks, monographs and treatises, the number of volumes is legion. They range from pamphlets and paperbacks dealing exhaustively with a single issue – or even a single stamp that has been studied in great depth – to monumental works such as the many-volumed handbooks on New Zealand and Hungary, published by the leading societies in the respective countries. Lower down the scale are the numerous books discussing the stamps of a country in more general terms and providing a useful overall survey for the collector who is perhaps contemplating taking up some new area of philately. Of particular use to the beginner are the many glossaries and dictionaries of philatelic terms, and here again Stanley Gibbons is pre-eminent with the splendid, all-colour guide entitled *Philatelic Terms Illustrated*. Gibbons also publishes a range of inexpensive guides to collecting thematics, postal history, writing up a collection, and even hints on competitive exhibiting. Mention has already been made of the American Topical Association whose range of titles now covers all the popular stamp collecting themes.

Periodicals
Philately supports a surprisingly large number of periodicals. In Britain alone there are five monthlies and a weekly of general interest, not to mention the monthly, bi-monthly or quarterly journals of the larger societies and the bulletins and newsletters of the specialist clubs and study circles. In addition, the British Philatelic Bureau publishes its own monthly *Philatelic Bulletin*, devoted to aspects of British stamps, past and present. Excellent bulletins of this kind are published by Guernsey, Jersey, India, Australia and New Zealand, and it seems likely that this idea will spread to other countries who currently produce brochures of new and forthcoming issues, themselves of immense value to the specialist for the information they contain. The more general periodicals contain news and views, articles on a wide variety of topics and a high proportion of advertising; whereas the more specialist publications have little or no advertising but contain the fruits of serious research. A regular subscription to one or more of the general magazines, as well as the relevant specialist periodicals (often free to members of the societies that publish them) should enable the serious collector to keep up to date with a hobby in which there is always something new, and with values that seem to be continually moving upwards.

Identification of stamps by their inscription

Most stamps can be identified by their inscription, language and expressions of value, but there are others that baffle even the collector of long standing. Below is a list of key-words and abbreviations found in inscriptions and overprints, with their country, state or district of origin.

A & T Annam and Tonquin
Açores Azores
Afghanes Afghanistan
Africa Portuguese Africa
Akahi Keneta Hawaii
Amtlicher Verkehr Württemberg
AO (Afrika Oost) Ruanda-Urundi
Allemagne/Duitschland Belgian occupation of Germany
A Payer/Te Betalen Belgium (postage due)
A Percevoir Belgium (franc and centimes); Egypt (paras, milliemes)
Archipel des Comores Comoro Islands
Avisporto Denmark
Azad Hind Free India (unissued stamps prepared for use in India after Japanese 'liberation')
B (on Straits Settlements) Bangkok
Bani (on Austrian stamps) Austrian occupation of Romania
BATYM Batum (now Batumi)
Bayer., Bayern Bavaria

BCA British Central Africa (now Malawi)
Belgique/België/Belgien, also Belge Belgium
Böhmen und Mähren Bohemia and Moravia
Bollo della Posta Napoletana Naples
Bosnien Bosnia
Braunschweig Brunswick
C CH Cochin China
Čechy a Morava Bohemia and Moravia
CEF (on India) Chinese Expeditionary Force
CEF (on German colonies) Cameroons under British occupation
Centesimi (on Austria) Austrian occupation of Italy
Centimes (on Austria) Austrian POs in Crete
Centrafricaine Central African Republic
Československo Czechoslovakia
Chiffre taxe France
Chine French POs in China
Comunicaciones Spain
Confed. Granadina Granadine Confederation (Colombia)
Cong Hoa Mien Nam National Liberation Front for South Vietnam
Congo Belge Belgian Congo
Continente Portuguese mainland
Corée Korea
Correio Brazil, Portugal
Correos Spain, Cuba, Porto Rico, Philippines
Côte d'Ivoire Ivory Coast

Côte Française des Somalis French Somali Coast
Danmark Denmark
Dansk Vestindien Danish West Indies
DDR German Democratic Republic
Deficit Peru
Deutsch Neu-Guinea German New Guinea
Deutsch Ostafrika German East Africa
Deutschösterreich Austria
Deutsch Südwestafrika German South West Africa
Deutsche Flugpost/Reichspost Germany
Deutsches Reich Germany
Dienstmarke Germany
Dienstsache Germany
Diligencia Uruguay
DJ Djibouti
Drzava, Drzavna Yugoslavia
EEF Palestine
Eesti Estonia
EE UU de C Colombia
EFO French Oceania
Eire Republic of Ireland
Elua Keneta Hawaii
Emp. Franç. French Empire
Emp. Ottoman Turkey
Equateur Ecuador
Escuelas Venezuela
España, Española Spain

Philatelic terms illustrated: bantams (South Africa); bisect (British Honduras); bilingual pair (South Africa); cancelled to order (North Borneo); control number (Great Britain); discount stamp and dominical label (both Belgium); gutter pair (France); printer's imprint (Southern Rhodesia); fiscal overprinted and surcharged for postal use (Nyasaland); phosphor bands (France); plate number (Germany); printer's waste (Haiti); tab (Israel); plate number (Israel); Red Cross (Bahamas); reprint (Buenos Aires); plate flaw (Queensland); roulette (Greece); provisional surcharge (New Zealand); tête-bêche triangular (Poland); anaglyptic or three dimensional (Italy); se-tenant pair (Germany), war tax (Bahamas) (66%)

Estados Unidos de Nueva Granada Colombia
Estensi Modena
Estero Italian POs in the Levant
Etablissements de l' Inde French Indian Settlements
Etablissements de l' Océanie French Oceanic Settlements
Etat. Ind. du Congo Congo Free State
Filipinas Spanish Philippines
Franco Switzerland
Francobollo Italy
Franco Marke Bremen
Franco Poste Bollo Neapolitan provinces and early Italy
Franqueo Peru
Franquicia Postal Spain
Freimarke Württemberg, Prussia
Frimerke Norway
Frimærke Denmark
G (on Cape of Good Hope) Griqualand West
G & D Guadeloupe
GEA Tanganyika
Gen. Gouv. Warschau German occupation of Poland
General Gouvernement German occupation of Poland
Georgie Georgia
Giuba Jubaland
GPE Guadeloupe
GRI British occupation of New Guinea and Samoa
Grossdeutsches Reich Nazi Germany
Guine Portuguese Guinea
Guinea Ecuatorial Equatorial Guinea
Guinée French Guinea
Gültig 9 Armee German occupation of Romania
Guyane Française French Guiana
Haute Volta Upper Volta
Helvetia Switzerland
HH' Nawab Shah Begam Bhopal
Hrvatska Croatia
HRZGL Holstein
IEF Indian Expeditionary Force
IEF 'D' Mosul
Imper. Reg. Austrian POs in Turkey
Impuesto de Guerra Spain (war tax)
Inde French Indian Settlements
India Port. Portuguese India
Irian Barat West Iran
Ísland Iceland
Jubilé de l'Union Postale Switzerland
Kamerun Cameroons
Kalatdlit Nunat, Kalaallit Nunaat Greenland
Kärnten Carinthia
Karolinen Caroline Islands
KGCA Carinthia
Kgl. Post. Frm. Denmark, Danish West Indies
Khmere Cambodia
Kongeligt Post Frimærke Denmark
KK Post Stempel Austria, Austrian Italy
KPHTH Crete
Kraljevina, Kraljevstvo Yugoslavia
Kreuzer Austria
KSA Saudi Arabia
K. u. K. Feldpost Austrian military stamps
K. u. K. Militärpost Bosnia and Herzegovina
K. Württ. Post Württemberg
La Canea Italian POs in Crete
La Georgie Georgia
Land-Post Baden
Lattaquié Latakia
Latvija Latvia
Lietuvos Lithuania
Litwa Środkowa Central Lithuania
Ljubljanska Pokrajina Slovenia
L. McL. Trinidad (Lady McLeod stamp)
Lösen Sweden

Magyar Hungary
MAPKA Russia
Marianen Mariana Islands
Maroc French Morocco
Marruecos Spanish Morroco
Mejico Mexico
Militär Post Bosnia and Herzegovina
Moçambique Mozambique
Modenesi Modena
Montevideo Uruguay
Moyen-Congo Middle Congo
MViR German occupation of Romania
Nachmarke Austria
Napoletana Naples
NCE New Caledonia
Nederland The Netherlands
Ned. Antillen Netherlands Antilles
Ned./Nederl. Indië Dutch East Indies
NF Nyasaland Field Force
Nippon Japan
Nieuwe Republiek New Republic (South Africa)
Nlle Caledonie New Caledonia
Norddeutscher Postbezirk North German Confederation
Norge/Noreg Norway
Nouvelle Calédonie New Caledonia
Nouvelles Hébrides New Hebrides
NSB Nossi-Bé (Malagasy)
NSW New South Wales
NW Pacific Islands North West Pacific Islands (New Guinea)
NZ New Zealand
Oesterr., Oesterreich, Österreich Austria
Off [*entlig*] *Sak* Norway (official stamps)
Oltre Giuba Jubaland
Orts Post Switzerland
OS Norway (official stamps)
Ottoman, Ottomanes Turkey
P, PGS Perak (Government Service)
Pacchi Postale Italy (parcel stamps)
Pakke-Porto Greenland
Para Egypt, Serbia, Turkey, Crete
Parm [*ensi*] Parma
Pesa (on German) German POs in Turkey
Piaster German POs in Turkey
Pilipinas Philippines
Pingin Ireland
Poblact na hEirann Republic of Ireland
Poczta Polska Poland
Pohjois Inkeri North Ingermanland
Port Cantonal Switzerland (Geneva)
Porte de Conducción Peru
Porte Franco Peru
Porte de Mar Mexico
Porteado Portugal and colonies
Porto Austria, Yugoslavia
Porto-pflichtige Württemberg
Post & Receipt/Post Stamp Hyderabad
Postage and Revenue United Kingdom
Postas le n'ioc Republic of Ireland
Postat e Qeverries Albania
Poste Estensi Modena
Poste Locale Switzerland
Postes Alsace and Lorraine, Belgium, Luxemburg
Poste Shqiptare Albania
Postgebiet Ob. Ost. German Eastern Army
Postzegel The Netherlands
Preussen Prussia
Provincie Modenesi Modena
Provinz Laibach Slovenia
PSNC Pacific Steam Navigation Co., Peru
Qeverries Albania
R Jind
Rayon Switzerland
Recargo Spain

Regno d'Italia Venezia Giulia Trieste
Reichspost German Empire
RF France and colonies
RH Haiti
Repoblika Malagasy Malagasy Republic
Republica Oriental Uruguay
Répub. Franç. France
République Libanaise Lebanon
République Rwandaise Rwanda
Rialtas Sealadac na hEireann Provisional Government of Ireland
RO Eastern Rumelia
Rumänien (on German) German occupation of Romania
Russisch-Polen German occupation of Poland
Sachsen Saxony
Scrisorei Moldavia and Wallachia
Segnatasse Italy
Serbien Austrian or German occupation of Serbia
SH Schleswig-Holstein
SHS Yugoslavia
Shqipenia, Shqipenië, Shqypnija, Shqiptare Albania
Sld., Soldi Austrian Italy
Slesvig Schleswig
Slovensky Stat Slovakia
SO Eastern Silesia
SPM St Pierre and Miquelon
S. Thomé e Principe St Thomas and Prince Islands
Suidwes Afrika South West Africa
Sul Bolletina, Sulla Ricevuta Italy
Sultanat d' Anjouan Anjouan
Suomi Finland
Sverige Sweden
SWA South West Africa
TAKCA Bulgaria
Tassa Gazzette Modena
Te Betalen Port Netherlands and colonies
TEO Cilicia, Syria
Terres Australes et Antarctiques Françaises French Southern and Antarctic Territories
Territoire Français des Afars et des Issas French Territory of the Afars and Issas
Tjänste Frimärke Sweden
Tjeneste Frimerke Norway
Tjeneste Frimærke Denmark
Toga Tonga
Toscano Tuscany
UAE United Arab Emirates
UAR United Arab Republic (Egypt)
UG Uganda
UKTT United Kingdom Trust Territory (Southern Cameroons)
Uku Leta Hawaii
Ultramar Cuba, Porto Rico
UNEF Indian Forces in Gaza
UNTEA Western New Guinea
Vallées d' Andorre Andorra
Van Diemen's Land Tasmania
Venezia Giulia (on Italian stamps) Trieste
Venezia Tridentina Trentino
Viet Nam Dan Chu Cong Hoa North Vietnam
Vom Empfänger Einzuziehen Danzig (postage due)
YCCP Ukraine
YKP. H. P. Ukraine
Z Armenia
ZAR South African Republic (Transvaal)
Z. Afr. Republiek South African Republic (Transvaal)
Zeitungsmarke Austria, Germany (newspaper stamps)
Zil Eloine Sesel Seychelles Outer Islands
Zuid West Afrika South West Africa
Zulassungsmarke German military parcel stamp

Glossary of philatelic terms

Stamp collectors have a language all of their own, which is often puzzling to the newcomer but many of the expressions are universally understood. Below are given some of the more commonly used terms, with their meanings.

Adhesive A stamp issued with gum on the reverse for sticking on mail, as opposed to one printed directly on the envelope, card or wrapper.

Aerogramme Specially printed air letter sheet on lightweight paper.

Airgraph Second World War forces mail sent by microfilm, then enlarged for dispatch to the addressee.

Albino A colourless impression, usually in embossing.

Alphabets The different styles of lettering printed in the corners of British stamps, 1840–87.

Anaglyptography Optical illusion creating a three-dimensional effect, used in Austrian stamps of 1890–1904.

Anaglyph Slightly misaligned image in red and green which, when viewed through special spectacles, gives a three-dimensional effect. Used for Italian stamps of 1956.

Backstamp Postmark on the back of an envelope, usually applied in transit or arrival.

Bantams South African stamps printed in a reduced format during the Second World War to save paper.

Bilingual pairs Stamps printed alternately in two different languages, e.g. South Africa (1926–50) and Ceylon (1964).

Bisect Stamp cut in half for use as a stamp of half the usual value, in times of shortage. Bisection may be made horizontally, vertically or diagonally.

Bleute paper Paper blued by chemicals in the printing ink or in the ingredients used in its manufacture.

Blind perforation Perforation in which the paper is merely dented, owing to blunt teeth in the perforating machine.

Block Four or more stamps joined together; also used in Europe as a synonym for a miniature sheet (q.v.).

Bogus Label purporting to be a genuine stamp but without any validity or even a reason for issue other than to defraud collectors. Bogus overprints may be found on genuine stamps for the same reason.

Burelage Pattern of fine lines incorporated in many stamp designs as a security feature.

Cachet A mark applied to cards and covers, other than the postmark and often private or unofficial in nature.

Cancellation Postmark applied to stamps to prevent their re-use. Usually hand- or machine-struck from steel or brass stamps, but may be of rubber, cork or wood, or even in pen and ink.

Cancelled to order (CTO) Stamps postmarked in bulk, usually for sale to philatelists below face value; usually recognized by still having the gum on the backs.

Cantonals The earliest issues of Switzerland (e.g. Basle, Geneva and Zürich).

Carriers Stamps issued by private carriers, mainly in the United States, 1842–59.

Centred Stamp whose design is equidistant from the edges of the perforations is said to be well centred. Off-centre stamps have the

perforations or scissor cuts (imperforate) cutting into the design on one or more sides.

Chalk-surfaced paper Security paper used for many British and colonial stamps to prevent re-use by cleaning off the cancellations. Can be detected by means of a silver pencil.

Chalky paper Special paper with a glossy surface used for many modern British definitive stamps, and also widely used for multicoloured stamps.

Chalon heads Name given to some early stamps of the Bahamas, Ceylon, New Zealand, Tasmania etc. reproducing a full-face portrait of Queen Victoria by Edward Chalon, RA.

Changeling Stamp whose colour has radically altered through immersion in water or exposure to sunlight.

Classics The earliest stamps of the world, 1840–1870.

Cliché Stereo or electro unit used in letterpress printing.

Coils Stamps issued in reels or coils and often collected in strips (q.v.). Can often be identified by being imperforate (q.v.) on two opposite sides.

Colour trials Proofs (q.v.) in various colours prior to issue, for the purpose of determining the most suitable colours in actual production.

Combination cover Cover bearing stamps of two or more postal administrations, mainly from the early period when stamps had no franking validity beyond the frontiers of the country of issue.

Comb perforation Stamps perforated on three sides at one stroke of the perforator have perfectly even corner teeth, compared with line perforation (q.v.).

Compound perforation Perforations of different gauges on different sides of the same stamp, e.g. British stamps are perf. 15 horizontally and 14 vertically.

Controls Letters and numerals found on British sheet margins, 1881–1947, for accounting purposes.

Corner block Stamps from the corner of the sheet, usually in 2 × 2 or 2 × 3, with marginal paper showing controls (q.v.), cylinder numbers (q.v.), plate numbers (q.v.) or printer's imprint (q.v.).

Cork cancellation Obliterators cut from corks, usually with fancy devices; widely used by nineteenth-century American postmasters. Sometimes used in Britain to obliterate incorrect datestamps.

CTO Widely used abbreviation for 'Cancelled to order' (q.v.).

Corner letters Double alphabet sequence of letters found in the corners of British stamps, 1840–87, and the first issues of Victoria.

Cover Envelope or wrapper with stamps affixed or imprinted. Stamps are said to be 'on cover' when the envelope is intact, as opposed to 'on front' or 'on piece'.

Cut-square or *Cut-out* Imprinted stamps cut from postal stationery; collected thus in America but whole items preferred elsewhere.

Cut to shape Imperforate stamps of unusual shapes, with margins trimmed accordingly.

Cylinder number Tiny numeral printed in the sheet margin to denote the cylinder(s) used in production.

Dandy roll Cylinder of wire gauze used in the manufacture of paper and associated with the impregnation of watermarks (q.v.).

Definitives Stamps in general use over a period of years, as opposed to commemoratives, charity stamps and other special issues.

Demonetized Obsolete stamps that have been declared invalid for postage.

Die The original piece of metal on which the stamp design is engraved.

Die proof An impression pulled from the die to check its accuracy.

Doctor blade Blade that removes surplus ink from photogravure cylinders as they revolve. Faulty adjustment may result in a white or coloured line running across the sheet of stamps.

Dominical labels Small labels attached below Belgian stamps, 1893–1914, instructing the postmen not to deliver the letter on Sunday. Where no objection was raised the labels were detached. Similar inscriptions may be found on Belgian postal stationery.

Dumb cancellation Postmarks with the town name erased for security reasons in wartime, and also special anonymous obliterations produced for the same purpose.

Duty plate Plate used to print the 'duty' (i.e. the value) in conjunction with the key plate (q.v.), a different duty plate being required for each denomination.

Engine-turning The intricate pattern of spiral lines forming the background to the earliest British and colonial stamps. A security device copied from contemporary banknotes.

Entire Complete envelope, card or wrapper.

Entire letter Complete envelope or wrapper, with the original contents intact.

Embossed Stamps, or a portion of their design, die-struck in low relief, often albino (q.v.) against a coloured background. Widely used for postal stationery.

Error Stamps deviating from the normal in some respect: missing or inverted colours, surcharges (q.v.) and overprints (q.v.) or mistakes in the design which may later be corrected. Errors are usually worth more than normals, but when the American Hammarskjöld stamp was found with the yellow colour inverted the USPO printed millions of errors for sale to collectors in order to minimize the rarity of the original.

Essay Preliminary design, not subsequently used.

Fake A genuine stamp that has been tampered with in some way to make it more valuable: e.g. fiscally used high-value stamps with the pen markings erased and a postmark substituted, or a stamp converted to a valuable rarity by the addition of an overprint.

First Day Cover or *FDC* Envelope bearing stamps used on the first day of issue.

First Flight Cover Cover carried on first airmail by a new route, or new aircraft.

Fiscal Stamp intended for fiscal or revenue purposes.

Flaw Defect in the printing plate or cylinder, resulting in a constant blemish on the same stamp in every sheet; plate flaws are useful in sheet reconstruction.

Frank A mark or label indicating that a letter or card can be transmitted free of postage. Widely used by government departments. Military franks have been issued by France, Vietnam etc. for use by servicemen.

Granite paper Paper containing tiny coloured fibres.

Graphite lines Black lines on the back of some British stamps, 1957–59, to do with electronic sorting experiments at Southampton. Superseded by phosphor bands (q.v.).

Grille Rectangular pattern of tiny squares embossed on some early stamps of Peru and the United States, to assist the cancelling ink to penetrate the paper thoroughly.

Gum The mucilage on the back of unused stamps. British stamps changed from gum arabic (glossy) to polyvinyl alcohol gum (matt, colourless) and now use PVA Dextrin gum (with a greenish tint).

Gutter Area between panes of a sheet. Stamps from adjoining panes with the gutter between are known as gutter or inter-panneau pairs.

Harrow perforation Process whereby an entire sheet is perforated at a single stroke, used notably by Austria and Hungary.

Healths Stamps issued by New Zealand, 1929 onwards, and Fiji (1951 and 1954), with a premium in aid of children's health camps.

Imperforate Stamps issued without any means of separating them, thus requiring them to be cut apart with scissors. Stamps with no perforations on one or more sides may come from booklets and those with no perforations on two opposite sides are from coils (q.v.).

Imprint Inscription giving the name or trademark of the printer. An imprint block is a block of four or more stamps with marginal paper attached bearing the imprint.

Interrupted perforation Dutch coil stamps with gaps in the perforation, intended to strengthen the coil and prevent the stamps accidentally tearing apart.

Inverts Stamps with a portion of the design upside down in relation to the rest.

Ivory head British 1d and 2d stamps of 1841 with the Queen's head showing up in white against a blue surround on the back, due to chemicals in the printing ink.

Jubilee line Lines of printer's rule reinforcing the edges of the plate and first used on the British 'Jubilee' series of 1887. Appears as bars of colour in the margin at the foot of the sheet.

Killer Cancellation designed to obliterate the stamp very heavily.

Kiloware Originally sealed kilo bags of stamps on paper, but now applied to any mixtures sold by weight.

Laminated prismatic printing Process used in some stamps of Bhutan to create a three-dimensional effect.

Locals Stamps whose validity is restricted to a single town or district and cannot be used for national or international mail.

Maltese cross Name erroneously given to the obliterators used in 1840–44 to cancel British stamps and struck in red, black and (much more rarely) other colours.

Marginal markings Marks on the margins of sheets include controls, cylinder and plate numbers, 'traffic lights', printers' imprints, jubilee lines (q.v.) sheet serial numbers, arrows showing the middle of the sheet, values of rows or sheets, ornament and even commercial advertising (France, Germany).

Meter marks Marks applied by a postage meter used by firms and other organizations. They comprise the indicium (or imitation 'stamp' with the value), the town die (with the date) and an advertising slogan, or may combine these elements in a single design. Invented in New Zealand (1904) and used internationally since 1922.

Miniature sheet Small sheet containing a single stamp or a small group of stamps, often with decorative margins.

Mint Unused stamp with full, original gum on the back.

Obsolete Stamps no longer on sale at the post office but still valid for postage.

Obliteration Postmarking of stamps to prevent re-use, synonymous with cancellation.

Omnibus issue Commemoratives issued by several countries simultaneously, using similar designs.

Overprint Printing applied to a stamp some time after the original printing, to convert it to some other purpose (e.g. commemorative, charity, or for use in some other country).

Pane Originally a portion of a sheet (half or quarter) divided by gutters (q.v.), but also applied to the blocks of stamps issued in booklets.

Patriotics Covers and cards with patriotic motifs, fashionable during the American Civil War, the Boer War and both world wars.

Pen cancellation Though mainly associated with fiscal use (q.v.) stamps postally used are known with this form of obliteration, notably from Scotland, Tasmania and Fiji. Modern stamps obliterated by ballpoint, having missed machine cancellation, are of no value.

Perfins Stamps perforated with initials or other devices as a security measure to prevent pilfering or misuse by office staff.

Perforation Form of separation using machines which punch out tiny circles of paper.

Phosphor bands Almost invisible lines on the face of stamps, to facilitate electronic sorting.

Plate Flat or curved piece of metal from which stamps are printed.

Plebiscites Stamps issued in towns and districts, mainly after the First World War, pending the vote of the population to decide which country they should join, e.g. Memel, Marienwerder, Carinthia and Silesia.

Poached eggs Nickname given to labels used by the British Post Office to test that vending machines were operating properly.

Postage dues Labels denoting the amount of postage unpaid or underpaid (often including a fine).

Postage Paid Impressions (PPIs) Marks printed on envelopes etc. used in bulk posting.

Postal stationery Envelopes, cards and wrappers bearing imprinted or embossed stamps.

Pre-cancels Stamps used in bulk postings, with marks previously overprinted to prevent re-use. Widely used by Canada, Belgium, United States and France, but now largely superseded by meter marks (q.v.) and postage paid impressions (q.v.).

Printer's waste Stamps with defective, double or misaligned printing, usually imperforate, and discarded during stamp production. Though usually strictly controlled, such material occasionally comes on to the market and is of interest to the specialist.

Provisionals Stamps overprinted (q.v.) or surcharged (q.v.) to meet a shortage of regular issues. Also used by emergent nations pending a supply of distinctive stamps, the stamps of the former mother country being overprinted.

Recess printing Term used in catalogues to signify intaglio printing.

Re-entry Portion of an intaglio plate which is re-engraved or re-entered by the transfer roller, usually detected by slight doubling of the lines.

Redrawn Stamps in which the basic design has been retained but various changes made in a subsequent edition.

Remainders Stocks of stamps on hand after an issue has been demonetized (q.v.) are sometimes sold off cheaply to the philatelic trade, with some form of cancellation to distinguish them from unused stamps sold at full value during the currency of the stamps.

Reprints Stamps printed from the original plates, sometimes long after the issue has ceased. They can be detected by differences in the paper, watermark and colour.

Retouch Repairs to letterpress plates and photogravure cylinders to touch out a flaw may result in stamps that can still be detected as slightly different from the normal, such corrections being known as retouches.

Rouletting Form of separation in which serrated instruments cut or pierce the paper without actually removing any, as in perforation (q.v.).

Secret marks Tiny letters, numbers, dates and other devices incorporated in the design of some stamps (notably the United States and Canada) for security reasons.

Selvedge Stamp edging or sheet marginal paper.

Se-tenant Two or more stamps of different designs, values or colours, printed side by side.

Specimen Stamp perforated or overprinted thus, or its equivalent in other languages, for record or publicity purposes and having no postal validity.

Straight edge Stamps with no perforations on one or more sides, mainly from coils and booklets but including sheets from such countries as Canada and the United States.

Surcharge An overprint (q.v.) that alters the face value of a stamp.

Tabs Stamps with marginal inscriptions alluding to the subjects depicted, widely used by Israel and also by Switzerland and the United Nations.

Taille douce French term sometimes used as a synonym for recess printing (q.v.).

Tête-bêche French term denoting two adjoining stamps, upside down in relation to each other.

Tied Postmarks that overlap the stamp and the envelope or card, a useful feature in establishing the genuineness of bisects (q.v.).

Typography Collector's term for letterpress printing, abbreviated in catalogues to 'typo'.

Unused Stamp without a cancellation, but in less perfect condition than mint (q.v.).

Used Stamp with a cancellation.

Variety Any variation from the normal issue, in shade, perforation, watermark, gum or phosphorescence, ignored by the simplified general catalogues, but listed in the more specialized works.

Vignette The main motif or central portion of a stamp design, as opposed to the frame, value tablet or inset portrait of the ruler.

Watermark Translucent impression used as a security device in the paper from which stamps are printed.

War tax Stamps thus inscribed or overprinted denote additional charges levied in wartime.

Woodblocks Nickname given to the rather crudely printed triangular stamps of Cape of Good Hope, 1861, although they were produced from metal clichés (q.v.). Actual woodblocks have been used to print stamps used by Polish prisoners of war, and some emergency issues in postwar Germany.

Zemstvos Russian locals (q.v.) prepaying postage from many towns to the nearest Imperial post office.

Zero stamps Spanish stamps with zero serial numbers on the reverse were used like specimens (q.v.) for record and publicity purposes.

Acknowledgments

The publishers would like to thank the following:
Bradbury & Wilkinson Co. Limited, New Malden, Surrey, England: 44 (above)
Mary Evans Picture Library, Blackheath, London: 1, 4, 28 (below)
Maurice Gale of the Cameo Stamp Centre, 75 Strand, London WC2: 38 (both), 41 (both), 71
Harrisons & Sons (High Wycombe) Limited: 44 (below), 46 (both)
Michael Holford Library, London: 7 (centre left)
Raymond Kaye for editorial work
The Mansell Collection, London: 7 (below), 8 (below), 28 (above)
The National Portrait Gallery, London: 8 (top left)
The Post Office has kindly given the Rainbird Publishing Group Ltd, permission to reproduce the Great Britain stamps
Vera Trinder Ltd, London: title-page, 40, 41 (bottom right), 74
Warwick & Warwick (Philately) Limited, Warwick: 10 (both), 72, 73 (both)

Index

Figures in **bold** type refer to illustrations

adhesive stamps, first 8–11
  tax 61
Adsons 64
aerial propaganda leaflets 30
aerogramme *see* air letters
aerophilately 28–31
airgraphs 30, 78
air letters 26–7, **27**, 28
airmail 28–31
  catalogues 75
  labels **62**, 63
air stamps 28, **29**, 29–30, **31**
  special delivery **3**h, 37
albums **40**, 40–1, 66, **66**
anaglyph **76**, 78
annotation 66–7, **67**
auctions 70–2

balloon mail **28**, 28–9, 30
bantams **76**, 78
bilingual pairs **76**, 78
billets de port payé 9
bisect **76**, 78
BM marks *see* MB marks
bogus stamps 58–9, **59**, 78
booklets 24–5, **24**, **25**, 75
  buying 72
  commemorative 25
  printing of **44**
  Wedgwood 42
British Guiana 1856 One Cent 48, 71
British Philatelic Exhibition 73
buying stamps 38, 70–2

cancellations 54–7, 78
  cork 78
  dumb 79
  FPO **27**, 57
  pen 79
cancelled to order (CTO), **76**, 78
catalogues 50, **74**, 74–5
Cavallini 9
CEPT 18–19
Chalmers, James 9
charity
  seals 59–60, **60**,
  stamps 20–3, **21**, **22**, **23**, 25
Christmas
  seals 59–60

stamps 18, **18**, 50
clubs, stamp 68–9
coils **24**, 25, 43, 78
colour 42
  code (UPU) 11
  printing **47**
  trials 78
commemorative
  booklets 25
  cards 26
  covers **13**
  sheets 24
  stamps **12**, 14–17, **14**, **15**, **16**, 48
condition 39
control numbers **76**, 78
covers 54, 78
  combination 78
  commemorative **13**
  first-day (FDCs) 55
  first-flight 30, 79
  mounting 67
  removing stamps from **39**
  souvenir **56**, **57**
cuneiform tablet **7**
cylinder numbers **42**, 47, 65

datestamps 6, 54–5
dealers 70
definitives 10–13
  airmail 28
  Elizabethan **48**
  pictorial **13**
  sheets 24
  United States **11**, 12
  see also booklets *and* coils
De La Rue 10, 24, 42, 44, 47
Departmentals 35

Easter stamps 18
embossed
  stamps 10, 26, **45**, 79
  stationery 8, 9, 14–15
  tax stamps 8, 61
embossing 45–6
errors **64**, 79
etiquettes **62**, 63
Europa issues 18–19, **19**
exhibitions 73
express delivery
  labels 63, **63**
  stamps 37, **37**

first-day covers (FDCs) 55, **55**, 75
fiscals 36–7, **61**, 61–2, **76**
flaws 64–5, **76**, 79
forgeries 59

General Letter Office 6
General Postal Union 7
General Post Office 6
Gray, Dr John 68
gutter pairs 24, **76**, 79

half-tone 45, 46
handstamps 55, **55**
handstruck marks 6, 8, 54
Harrison and Sons 46, 47
'healths' 22, 25, **55**, 79
helicopter mail 30–1
Hill, Sir Rowland 8, **8**, 9, 51
hinges **41**
horses on stamps 52

imprint, printer's **76**, 79
inscriptions 76–7
insurance stamps 62
intaglio 44, 45, 64
interpanneau pairs *see* gutter pairs

joint issues 19
journal tax stamps 34
jubilee lines **42**, 47, 79

keyplates 12, 16
kiloware 38, **39**
Košir (Koschier), L. 9

labels 59–60, 62–3, **62**, **63**, 65

dominical **76**, 79
local carriage 58
postage-due 32–3
registration 37, 62, **62**
layout, album page 66–7
letter
  cards 27
  sheets 9, 26, 28
letterpress 10, 44–5, 65
letters
  air 26–7, **27**
  pre-stamp 6, **6**, 7, 54
  ship 56
line-engraveds 10
line engraving 10, 44
lithography 45, 65
  offset 45, 46, 47

magnifiers 41, **41**
Maltese Cross **8**, 54, 79
maximum cards 55–6
MB marks 56
meter marks 8, 79
military mails 57
miniature sheets 25, **47**, 79
  catalogues 75
mounting strips 41, 66, **67**
Mulready envelopes 8, **8**
museum collections 69

National Philatelic Centre 71, **72**, **73**
newspaper
  stamps 34, **34**, **35**
  wrappers 27, 34
New Year stamps 18
Norden 18

obliterators 54–5
obsolete stamps 49
official mails 34–6
Olympic stamps 16–17, 50
omnibus issues **15**, 16, **16**, 18–19, 52
overprints 15, 34–6, 76–7, 79

Paisley Rocketeers 31
paper 42
Paquebot marks 56, **56**
parcel
  -post labels **63**
  stamps 34–5, 36
Penny Black 8, 10, **10**, 35, 65
  sheets 24
Penny Red 10, 65
perfins 35, 39, 79
perforations 43
periodicals 75
philatelic bureaux 72
phosphor 43, 64, **76**, 79
photogravure 46–7, **46**, 65
PHQ cards 27
pigeon posts 28, 30
plate numbers 47, **76**
plating 65
postage-dues 23, **32**, 32–4, 79
postal conventions 11
postal fiscals 36–7, **76**
postal history 54–7
  catalogues 75
  local 57
postal services 54
  history of 6–8
  private 58
postal stationery 8, 9, 14–15, 26–7, 45, 79
  buying 72
  catalogues 75
  commemorative 14
postal treaties 7, 11
postcards 26, **26**, 27, **27**
postcodes 55
postmarks 8, 54–7, 75
  pictorial **57**
  railway 56–7, **57**
  see also cancellations
presentation packs 27

printer's waste **76**, 79
private posts 58
Pro Juventute **20**, 20–1
Pro Patria 21, **21**
proofs 65, 75
provisionals **76**, 79
purpose-of-issue collecting 52–3

quartz lamp 43, 64

railway mails 56–7
  postmarks 56–7, **57**
  stamps **36**
recess printing 10
  see also intaglio
Red Cross 21–2, 23, 25
registered
  envelopes 26
  mail 37
registration
  labels 37, **62**
  stamps **32**, 37
reprints **76**, 79
revenues *see* fiscals
rocket mail 31, **31**
rouletting 43, **76**, 79

savings stamps 62
SCADTA stamps 29
sea mails 56
Seebeck, Nicholas 12
semi-postal stamps *see* charity stamps
se-tenant strips 25, **76**, 79
sheets 24, 25, 60, 65
ship letter 56
  mark **6**
special delivery
  labels 63, **63**
  stamps 37, **37**
special issues **14**, **17**, 17–19
sports stamps 16–17
Stampex 73
stickers 62–3
subject collecting 51–2
supranationals 49

tabs **76**, 79
tax stamps 23 *see also* fiscals
telegraph stamps 62, 75
telephone stamps 62
tête-bêche pairs 25, **76**, 79
thematic collecting 50–3
  annotation of 67
tongs *see* tweezers
topical collecting *see* thematic collecting
'traffic lights' 24, 47, 65
travelling post offices (TPOs) 56
tweezers 41, **41**
Twopence Blue 8, **10**
typesetting 44–5
typography *see* letterpress

Uniform Penny Postage 7, 8, 20
United Nations 18, 49, **49**
Universal Postal Union (UPU) 7, 11, 16, 62, 63
uprated items 27

Victoria, Queen
  Diamond Jubilee 15, 20
  head of, on stamps 9, **9**, 15
V-mail 30

war-tax stamps 23, **76**, 79
watermarks 25, 43
wing-margined stamps 24
wrappers 9, 26
  Mulready 8
  newspaper 27, 34
writing-up *see* annotation

Zemstvos 58, 79